仅以本书纪念已故露丝·巴德·金斯伯格大法官

In memory of Ruth Bader Ginsburg, former Associate Justice of

the Supreme Court of the United States

我想被铭记为一个竭尽所能、尽力而为的人。
——露思·巴德·金斯伯格

I would like to be remembered as someone who used whatever talent

she had to do her work to the very best of her ability.

——Ruth Bader Ginsburg

成长的法律烦恼

GROWING PAINS IN LAW

沈奕　沈宏山○著

Yi Shen | Hongshan Shen

复旦大学出版社

目录
Table of Contents

用法律呵护成长（序） 沈岿 ·················· 001
Growth Nurtured by Law（Foreword）　　Kui Shen

沈奕自序 ·················· 013
Preface by Yi Shen

沈宏山自序 ·················· 020
Preface by Hongshan Shen

第 一 章　我要上学 ·················· 026
Chapter 1　I Want to Go to School!

第 二 章　好心办坏事 ·················· 056
Chapter 2　Good Intention, Bad Outcome

第 三 章　收留"美少女" ·················· 085
Chapter 3　Adopting "Beauty"

| 第 四 章 | 乐不起来的胜利 | 116 |
| Chapter 4 | Sullen Victory | |

| 第 五 章 | 狗急跳墙 | 143 |
| Chapter 5 | A Cornered Beast Will Do Something Desperate | |

| 第 六 章 | 紧急避险 | 171 |
| Chapter 6 | Necessity | |

| 第 七 章 | 收回录取通知书 | 198 |
| Chapter 7 | Taking Back the Offer | |

| 第 八 章 | 黑色星期五 | 224 |
| Chapter 8 | Black Friday | |

| 第 九 章 | 正当防卫 | 256 |
| Chapter 9 | Right to Self Defense | |

| 第 十 章 | 我的作品我做主 | 288 |
| Chapter 10 | I'm in Charge of My Work! | |

用法律呵护成长（序）

欣然答应作序，不是因为我和两位作者共享同一个中国姓氏。或许，百年前、千年前，我们的祖先真的生活在同一大家族之中也未可知。眼下，我们却无任何亲缘关系。

欣然答应作序，也不是因为在书中以父亲身份出现的作者之一——沈宏山大律师——是我在本科期间的同学。我们曾经在博雅塔下、未名湖边、图书馆中（即著名的北大"一塔湖图"），共同度过四年的青葱岁月。

欣然答应作序，更多是因为三年前认识了本书的主创：沈奕——我更习惯称呼她的英文名 Emily（埃米莉）。记得那时，我带着9岁稚儿在美国费城的宾夕法尼亚大学访学一年，感恩节期间，驱车前往宏山家中相聚，遇见了埃米莉。这是我们初次见面，也是迄今唯一的一次见面，但欢快、懂事、喜好体育、热爱学习的埃米莉给我留下了非常深刻的印象。12岁的她大方地同我这个素未谋面的父亲同学聊天，带着我们在院子里一起打排球，把她亲手制作的茶托送给我们做纪念，并留下了十分秀丽的英文签名，吃完晚饭后，又很有礼貌地离席去跟同学在网上共同研究数学。

所以，当宏山提及埃米莉与他用了两年多时间，完成了一部记录他们曾经的法律探讨的小书时，我十分好奇，这个阳光少女会以什么方式，同我们分享什么样的成长故事呢？

身为父母的家长有权决定将孩子留在家里，不去学校接受教育吗？

好心帮助同学看管财物，不小心弄丢了，自己要赔偿同学的损失吗？

在路边捡到走失的小狗，悉心照料，不仅救了它，还陪伴它生下了更可爱的狗宝宝，培养了深厚情感，狗的主人可以说把它们带走就带走吗？

爱好排球并参加排球俱乐部的同学，代表俱乐部比赛受了重伤，治伤的巨额医疗费只能由同学及其家庭自己承担吗？

带着朋友同邻居家的狗玩耍，朋友不慎被狗咬伤了，朋友的治疗费用邻居家有责任赔偿吗？自己有责任赔偿吗？

为了救正在溺水、拼命挣扎的伙伴不得不将其打晕，却因为出手过重造成了伙伴的脑震荡，要为此承担什么后果吗？

学校发了录取通知书，自己已经为此举办过庆祝会，还拒绝了其他几家有意录取自己的学校，可是，学校又通知说是错发，要收回，学校有权这么做吗？

一家人在购物节去大超市购物，爸爸妈妈嘱咐自己临时照顾弟弟，弟弟却因商场地滑而摔骨折了，商场要不要支付医疗费用？

同学受到别的学校学生的霸凌，当场奋起反击，却用棒球棒把霸凌学生打伤，同学需要为此担责吗？

参加学校的绘画课，创作了一幅让老师非常满意的作品，并且在学校画廊上展示了，学校可以不事先经过自己的同意，把画作印制在学校的挂历上吗？

十个问题，带着浓厚的"法律之问"色彩，也就是关于谁有权利、谁有义务/责任的追问，由女主角艾莉的十个成长故事——有的甚至是梦中故事——一一牵引出来；作为律师的父亲和女儿艾莉之间，又展开了抽丝剥茧式、打破砂锅问到底式、请君入瓮下套式的提问、回答，对十个问题进行了饶有趣味的讨论。其中，一个有着仁爱之心、健康活泼、乐于助人、特别爱思考爱提问题的女生，一个循循善诱、愿意抽出时间陪伴女儿、由浅入深地搬出法律概念、原理的慈父，以及悄然隐身于父女背后却稳稳的、默默的、不可或缺的母亲，跃然纸上。

很显然，这些应该不是发生在埃米莉一家身上的真实故事，却处处可见他们——尤其是埃米莉——学习和生活的影子。而这些故事所牵扯的问题，相信是埃米莉父女之间真正讨论过的，相信也会是许多小读者和他们的家长们似曾相识地经历过、困惑过的。

我们生活在一个群体社会中,出生伊始就与"自我"以外的其他人——最初就是父母——打交道,很少会像鲁滨孙那样被困于一个孤岛。在严复[1]所称的"群己"关系中,我们持续不断地接受"应该怎样、不应该怎样"的教育,其中绝大多数事关如何待人接物。"应该怎样、不应该怎样"的叙述,其实隐然有权利与义务的内涵,只不过,有的是道德上的,有的是纪律上的,有的则是法律上的。正是各种各样的权利义务关系,构成了一个虽然错综复杂但又基本井井有条的社会秩序。

然而,我们的生活并不总是平和安宁的,人与人之间的利益冲突和纠葛在所难免。从童年到少年再到青年,发生在自己身上和周边的冲突和纠葛会愈来愈多,或者被愈来愈多地意识到,疑问和困惑也就常常伴随左右。这也许就是一个从"不识愁滋味"到"识尽愁滋味"[2]的过程。解决疑惑的视角、方法有多种,法律应该是其中最能细微区分差异情形中的权利义务配置的,如书中所提的父母对孩子的权利、商场对顾客的义务、正当防卫与防卫过当等,皆需付诸具体而微的情境进行分析。

一个人可以不选择法律作为自己学习研究的主科,但一个人绝不可能不与法律产生交集,绝不可能永远不用法律

---

[1] 严复(1854—1921)是清末及民国初年著名的教育家和翻译家。
[2] 摘自宋朝诗人辛弃疾的著名诗歌。

思考或解决遭遇的问题，也绝不可能在完全欠缺法律意识和知识的情况下真正"长大成人"——用学术一点的语言就是真正"社会化"和"教化"。我们的成长，我们孩子的成长，都需要法律的呵护，以及对这种呵护的足够认识。

小说体的叙事、苏格拉底式教学的问答、跨国界的情境（尤其体现在西方的人物姓名与中国的法律概念），以及中英文的对照文本，都是这本书引人入胜之处。相信小读者们会喜欢它，了解同样的故事和讨论在不同语言中是如何展开的，相信家长们也能从中汲取保护孩子、帮助孩子的法律知识，以及如何与孩子沟通类似困惑的方法。

热切期盼，眼前电脑中的文字、图画，早日转变为透着浓浓油墨香味的掌中书。

是为序。

沈 岿

北京大学法学院教授

2020 年 7 月 22 日

Growth Nurtured by Law
— Foreword

I readily agreed to write this foreword, not because I share the same Chinese last name (as in "Shen") with the two authors. Perhaps our families may be related through a common ancestor who lived hundreds or even thousands of years ago. However, for now, we must assume that we are not related.

I readily agreed to write this foreword, not because one of the authors who appears in the book as the father — Attorney Hongshan Shen — was an undergraduate classmate of mine. We spent four years together next to the Porter Tower and the Weiming Lake and in the Peking University Library (the famous PKU picture of "a tower, a lake, and a library" with homophonic pun in Chinese as "a picture of a mess").

Rather, I enthusiastically agreed to write this foreword because I met the main author of this book — Yi Shen — three years ago (although I am more used to calling her by her English name: Emily). In 2017, I was a visiting scholar at University of

Pennsylvania in Philadelphia and had brought my nine-year-old son with me during my tenure in the United States. During Thanksgiving of 2017, I drove to Hongshan's home for a visit and met Emily there. Emily left me with a deep impression as a cheerful, sophisticated, sports-loving, and curious young girl. Emily elegantly chatted with me — her father's classmate — who she had never met before, led us to play volleyball in the yard, and gave me a saucer she had made, complete with her beautiful English signature. After dinner, Emily left the table politely to study mathematics online with her classmates.

Needless to say, when Hongshan mentioned that Emily had spent more than two years with him to complete this little book that, in many ways, serves as a record of the legal discussions between them, I was very curious about how and what growth story Emily — this sunshine girl — would share with us.

Do parents have the right to decide for their children on whether they should be homeschooled or go to school for education?

When helping your classmate take care of his/her property, if you accidentally lose the property, do you have to compensate your classmate for the loss?

Suppose you found a lost puppy on the side of the road, kept the little puppy with you and took good care of it. Now not only have you saved her, but you also attended her when she gave birth to her baby dogs. During the process, you have cultivated sentiments and emotions for the puppy and her babies. Can the owner of the puppy just take them away from you?

For students who love volleyball and participate in volleyball clubs, suppose they played on behalf of the club and suffered serious injuries during the games, and the medical expenses were huge. Would the injured students and their families bear the expenses themselves?

You brought your friend to play with your neighbor's dog at the neighbor's home. Your friend was accidentally bitten by the dog. Should the neighbor be responsible for your friend's treatment expenses? Should you be responsible?

Suppose that in order to save your drowning and struggling mate, you didn't have any choice but to render him unconscious in order to stop his struggle. Though you saved him from drowning, you caused a concussion. Do you have to bear any consequence for this?

Suppose a school offered you a Letter of Admission. You celebrated for this offer and rejected several other schools' offers.

However, the school that offered admission then notified you that the letter was sent by mistake and was therefore revoked. Does the school have the right to do so?

Your family went to a big mall on Black Friday. Your mom and dad asked you to look after your younger brother while they shopped. However, your brother slipped near a fountain and suffered a fracture. Should the mall be responsible?

Suppose your classmate was being bullied by one student of another school. Your classmate fought back with a baseball bat after being provoked and injured the bullying student. Should the classmate take responsibility for this?

You participated in the school's painting class and created a painting which was satisfactory to your teacher. The painting was then displayed in the school gallery. Can the school print the painting on the school calendar without your prior consent?

Ten questions with strong legal tones — who has rights and who has obligations/responsibility — are drawn out one by one by ten growth or even dream stories of the heroine Ellie. Between the lawyer father and the daughter Ellie expand interesting and enlightening discussions on the ten questions: issue spotting and factual analysis through the lens of a dynamic Socratic dialogue. Ellie stands out as a kind, lively girl who enjoys helping others while also imbued with a deep intellectual curiosity. Her benevolent father encourages these questions and works to help her understand complex principles and concepts. Behind them is her supportive mother, who stands silently, steadily, yet indispensably and supports the family.

Obviously, these stories did not truly happen to Emily. Nevertheless, we can see vivid projections of Emily's study and life. As for the issues involved in these stories, I believe that Hongshan and Emily have had discussions regarding these kinds of scenarios, and I believe that many young readers and their parents will find the ways in which Ellie and her father discuss these confusing situations to be very familiar and helpful.

Rather than being stuck on an island like a version of Robinson, we live in a society based on complex relationships with others — in fact, our first set of relationships are with our parents. In what Fu Yan [1] calls a "group-self" (*qunji*) relationship, we continue to receive education about what should and should not be done, most of which are about how to deal with others. The narrative of "what should and should not be done" actually has connotations of rights and obligations, some of which are moral, some disciplinary, and some legal. A variety

---

[1] Fu Yan (1854–1921) was a very well-known educator and translator in the end of the Qing dynasty and the beginning of the Republic of China.

of rights and obligations constitute a social order that is intricate but basically well-organized.

However, our lives are not always peaceful and tranquil; conflicts of interest and entanglements between people are inevitable. The transitions from childhood to adolescence and then to adulthood involve learning how to identify and work through conflicts. This can be a very difficult and confusing process. This might be a shifting process from "not knowing any sorrowful taste" to "understanding all the sorrowful tastes."[1] There are many perspectives and methods for solving doubts and confusions. The law can serve as a guide by which we can finely distinguish the rights and obligations in different scenarios, just as laid out in this book: case by case, it analyzed the rights of parents over children, the duties of shopping malls owing to customers, legitimate defense and excessive defense, etc.

One may not choose law as the main subject of their own study and research; but one can never live completely without interacting with the law, never solve the problems encountered completely without using legal thinking, nor grow up or mature — in academic terms, "socialized" and "civilized" — completely without any legal awareness or knowledge. Our growth, and the

---

[1] The quotes are verses from a famous poem written by poet Qiji Xin in the Song dynasty.

growth of our children, needs to be nurtured by the law, and we need to adequately acknowledge the nurture as well.

Fictional narratives, Socratic Q&A, the transnational context (especially reflected in the western names of the characters and the Chinese legal concepts), and the bilingual texts, are all what make this book fascinating and intriguing. I believe that young readers will love it, and they would be interested to know how the same stories and discussions are narrated in different languages. I believe that parents can also learn from this book some legal knowledge to protect, help, and nurture their children, and explore a way to discuss similar confusions with their children.

I am thrilled and cannot wait to see the texts and pictures right from the screen of my laptop to be transformed into a book with a strong ink fragrance.

Such is my foreword.

Kui Shen
Professor, Peking University Law School
July 22, 2020

沈奕自序

我接触法律大概是从幼儿园大班开始的!

一天,老师给我们每个小朋友布置了一项作业:回家了解自己爸爸或者妈妈的工作,两天后幼儿园将举办"职业日"活动。

放学回家的路上,我牵着爸爸的手,吃着棒棒糖,听着爸爸绘声绘色地讲他工作中的"奇闻逸事"。我禁不住问:"爸爸,律师的工作都干些什么,是不是乘着飞机到处玩呀?"

听到我的话,爸爸哈哈大笑,顿了顿,说:"爸爸有很多朋友,当他们遇到麻烦事儿时,爸爸就会去帮忙。"听得出,想把"法律"这个职业用简单的语言解释给一个六岁的孩子听还真不是一件容易的事儿。

听到这个解释,我心里悄悄地把"律师"和"超人"画上了等号。在我幼小的心目中,他们都是保护弱者、维护正义的人。我经常想象,爸爸就是电视剧里那个专门对付坏人的英雄,有了"爸爸",人们就可以幸福快乐地生活。我在心里暗下决心,长大以后自己也要成为这样的人。

于是，一有时间我就缠着爸爸给我讲法律故事，并且特别愿意猜每个法律故事的结果，以此为乐！慢慢地，我也把学校里同学们遇到的一些法律问题讲给爸爸听，和爸爸一起讨论。这些故事和讨论滋养着我一路成长，更悄悄地开启了我研究法律问题的大门。到了今天，很多故事的内容已经依稀模糊，但是，夕阳下，一个小女孩牵着爸爸的手走在回家的路上听着爸爸讲故事的景象却深深地印在了我的心里、我的脑海里。

随着研究的深入，我对法律有了更多的理解。俗话说，国有国法，家有家规。其实法律就是一些最基本的规则，它告诉人们什么事能做，什么事不能做。正是因为有些人不遵守这些规则，我们的社会才会有伤害和被伤害。因此，不管怎样，我们首先要做一个遵守规则的人。

我从小练习排球，训练和比赛中磕磕碰碰时有发生，因此我和爸爸深入地讨论了运动员在比赛中受伤的法律责任问题。没过多久，我的队友在比赛中倒地救球，导致髋骨严重受伤。这让我深刻地认识到，法律并非只是成人世界的事，它离我们青少年并不遥远，它每天都可能发生在我们或我们身边的朋友身上。

我们知道，全世界有近三分之一的人口是青少年和儿童，每天都有很多青少年和儿童遭受到各种形式的伤害，这些伤害可能是身体上的，可能是精神上的，也可能是财产方面的。如果我们掌握一些法律知识，可能就能减轻甚至避免这些伤害。于是，我萌发了写本书的念头，想借此书与更多的青少年朋友分享我的研究和感悟，发现法律的魅力，喜欢上法律。同时，也希望青少年朋友能通过这本书学到一些法律知识，让自己强大起来，从而更好地保护自己，帮助他人！

写本序时正值新冠肺炎疫情在全球大流行，每天从媒体上听到或看到很多患者不幸离世的消息，更听到或看到很多在灾难面前人们勇敢互助、团结友爱的感人故事。人类学家玛格丽特·米德（Margaret Mead）说过，"从困难中帮助别人才是文明的起点"。我相信，只要我们携手相助，共克时艰，风雨后一定会再见彩虹！

感谢复旦大学出版社和编辑李荃老师，感谢沈岿教授、凯瑟琳·菲德勒（Katherine Fidler）博士，以及Yao/studio puke ink。你们的爱在这至暗时刻显得更加璀璨和温暖！

沈奕（埃米莉）

2020年3月

Preface by Yi Shen

I was first exposed to the concept of "law" when I was in the kindergarten!

One day, our kindergarten teacher assigned each of us a project: we had to learn about our parents' jobs in preparation for the upcoming "career day."

On our way home from kindergarten, I held my dad's hand, with a lollipop in my mouth, while listening to my dad talk about the exciting experiences he had at work. I couldn't help myself from asking, "Dad, what do lawyers do? Do they fly around on a plane and go on vacations?"

My dad laughed and said after a short pause, "Your dad has a lot of friends. When they run into trouble, I help them out." Looking back, I now understand that it is not easy to explain what law is to a six-year-old child.

After hearing this explanation, although I didn't fully understand it, I drew an equal sign between "lawyers" and "superheroes." In my six-year-old mind, both were people who protect the weak and uphold justice. I often imagined that Dad was the hero in the TV shows who made sure that villains were brought to justice. I secretly made up my mind, setting the goal that I would become a person just like Dad when I grow up.

After that first conversation, I would beg for my dad to tell me legal stories. I was especially eager to guess the verdict of each legal issue — it was so much fun! Gradually, I started telling my father about some legal issues that my classmates at school had encountered and discussed the possible outcomes with my father. These stories and discussions nourished my growth and quietly opened the door to my legal research journey. I can no longer recall the content of many of these stories, but the image of a little girl holding her father's hand on the way home as the sun was setting and listening to her father's stories is deeply imprinted in my mind and in my heart.

As I dove further into legal research, I gained a deeper understanding of what law is. As the adage goes, every nation has its own laws and every family has its own rules. In fact, laws are some of the most basic rules that tell people what are allowed and what are prohibited. Many of these laws are designed to make sure that people do not act in a way that harms others. Therefore, no matter what happens, we first need to be respectful citizens who follow the rules.

One of the first times that I realized that law does not merely exist in the adult world was in connection to a sports activity! I have been playing volleyball since I was little, and injuries during training and tournaments are inevitable. I remember discussing who might bear liability if a student athlete was injured during competitions. Not long after that abstract conversation, one of my teammates, while trying to dig the ball during a game, got a serious hip injury. This made me realize that law does not merely exist in the adult world. It is closer to teenagers than we thought, and it could happen to any of us or our friends any day.

Nearly one-third of the world's population consists of young adults and children. Every day, many young children suffer from various types of harm. These harms may be physical, mental, or financial. If more people, including young people, have a basic legal understanding, these injuries may be reduced or even prevented. This was the original idea behind the book: I wanted to share my research and insights with other teenagers and encourage them to discover the beauty of law and to like law. At the same time, I also hope that my teenage friends can learn about their legal rights and responsibilities so that they can better protect themselves and even help others!

This preface is written during the time of the COVID-19

epidemic around the world. Every day, I am updated with the news of new cases and unfortunate deaths of patients all over the world, and I am also touched by many stories of people bravely helping each other and uniting together by the power of love in the face of the crisis. Margaret Mead, a famous anthropologist, once said, "Helping someone else through difficulty is where civilization starts." I believe that as long as we work together to help overcome the difficult times, we will definitely see the rainbow after the storm!

I am beyond grateful for Fudan University Press and editor Ms. Quan Li, Professor Kui Shen, Dr. Katherine Fidler, and Yao/ studio puke ink. Your love and support are brighter and warmer than ever in this seemingly dark moment!

Best,
Yi Shen, Emily
March 2020

沈宏山自序

每一个父母都恨不得把自己知道的东西都告诉孩子,让孩子一下子长大,最好能变成自己的样子。作为一名律师,作为一名父亲,我也有意无意地给孩子讲讲自己的工作,讲讲法律,这可能就是孩子对法律产生兴趣的开始。

不过,埃米莉喜欢法律最初可能是出于好奇,甚至当成听故事,因此会提出无数在我看来无厘头甚至无法回答的问题。和所有父母一样,我一遍一遍地回答孩子看似重复的问题。现在看来,幸好当初没有放弃,否则就没有这篇冗长的自序了。

慢慢地,我发现孩子不但能听懂这些"枯燥"的法律,而且还能形成自己朴素的逻辑和推理,她的推理结果有时甚至非常接近正确答案。这让我惊叹孩子巨大的潜力和无限的可能,也让我意识到自己低估了孩子、高估了自己。

随着研究的深入,我们的讨论逐步聚焦到青少年生活中经常遇到的法律问题,比如:你在学校里被同学打伤了,你可以要求同学的家长承担责任吗?别人捡到了你丢失的东西,你可以要回来吗?等等。有一天,女儿兴奋地告诉我,她把我们讨论的故事讲给自己的朋友们听,有些故事居然就发生在他们身上,因此朋友们不但愿意听,而且很受益!从女儿坚定的语气中,我感受到了她的力量和成长。

当女儿提出想写本书与更多的孩子分享我们的讨论时,我像多数家长一样立刻欢呼雀跃,表示支持,但是内心却有些犹豫,因为我知道写书的过程是多么艰苦和漫长。果不其然,孩子写作过程中的一切烦躁、不安和日积月累的重复,我至今还历历在目。但是,幸运的是我当初没有拒绝孩子的提议,今天才能以这个特别的方式,记录我和孩子共同成长的岁月。

陪伴女儿研究以及和女儿共同写作的过程,看似是我带着女儿讨论和总结,其实更是孩子带着我成长。每每听着女儿绘声绘色地讲述她研究的法律案例或者分享她的研究心得,我都会深深地被她对未知领域探索的渴望和热情所感染,并催我奋进。由于研讨和写作的需要,我开始系统地关注世界儿童和青少年保护问题。受孩子的激励,我开始更多地和青年学生分享律师生活,探讨法律世界。我经常告诉自己,也许有一天这些孩子就会成长为律师或者法官,可以帮助到更多的人。所以,感谢女儿为我的生活开启了一扇门,打开了一扇窗,而且这里永远空气新鲜、生机勃勃!

亲爱的女儿,每个人都在他人铺就的台阶上前行,因此未来不管遇到什么样的困难,哪怕是遇到百年不遇的疫情,都要继续保持一颗柔软和悲悯的心,尽自己所能给周遭的人带去温暖和力量。

感谢复旦大学出版社,作为以出版学术专著著称的全球知名出版社,同意出版本书即是对其社会价值的认可,更是给予我和女儿最好的礼物!

沈宏山

2020 年 3 月

Preface by Hongshan Shen

One of the joys of parenthood is watching your children grow and develop their own interests and passions. When your child expresses an interest in what you do for work, that joy grows. As a lawyer and a father, I have always talked with my Emily about my work and the law, hoping that it might kindle her enthusiasm for the law.

Emily has demonstrated a curiosity about the law from an early age, raising all kinds of questions ranging from the serious to the silly! Like all parents, I worked to answer Emily's many questions and, looking back, I am so grateful that we had those early exchanges.

As time passed, I realized that my girl not only understood many of these "dreary" laws but was also forming her own reasoning skills. The outcome of her deduction was sometimes very close to the formal answer, and I marveled at Emily's potential in the legal field. I also realized that I might have underestimated my girl and overestimated myself.

As Emily's research process progressed, our discussions gradually concentrated on legal issues often encountered by juveniles. For example, if you were injured by a classmate at school, can you hold the classmate's parents accountable? One day, Emily excitedly informed me that she had shared with her friends several of the scenarios we had discussed. Not only were her friends curious to hear these stories, but they also benefited from the stories! From my daughter's firm tone, I was impressed with her strength and growth.

When Emily proposed that we write a book for children based on our discussions, I was thrilled and supportive. I also knew how hard the writing process would be and that it would be a significant learning experience for Emily. As expected, Emily experienced all the irritability, restlessness, and frustration that accompanies a project of this size! However, she pushed forward, and I am so happy that I encouraged her in this project. This book is also a very special record of the many conversations she and I had throughout her childhood.

When we first embarked on this project, I thought I would take the lead to discuss and summarize; in fact, my daughter also pushed me to grow and expand my knowledge. Whenever my daughter shared with me the scenarios or her growth from the research, I was always deeply impressed and touched by her desire and enthusiasm to explore unknown subject areas, and that was precisely what motivated and drove me forward. I began to focus systematically on child and juvenile protection around the world. Inspired by my girl, I started to share details of what a lawyer actually does with young students. I often tell myself that maybe one day these kids will grow into lawyers or judges who can offer help to many more. Therefore, I ought to thank my daughter for opening a door and a window in my life, where air is always fresh and vibrant!

Daughter, my dear, people always march on the steps paved by others; so, no matter what difficulties you may encounter in the future, even in the face of an epidemic unlikely to have occurred in a century, you must continue to maintain a soft and compassionate heart and do your best to bring warmth and strength to those around you.

We would like to acknowledge Fudan University Press. As a world-renowned publishing house, best-known for academic monographs, Fudan University Press' assent to publish this book is per se a recognition of its value, and it makes the best gift for my daughter and myself!

Hongshan Shen
March, 2020

第一章
我要上学

·导读·

阿丽莎的爸爸妈妈吵架,妈妈一气之下撇下阿丽莎和弟弟去了外婆家,爸爸不让阿丽莎上学,让她留在家里照顾弟弟。阿丽莎很想去学校上学,学校老师也三番五次地劝说阿丽莎的爸爸。阿丽莎重返学校的愿望能实现吗?父母有权不让孩子到学校读书吗?

艾莉和阿丽莎从小学一年级开始就是同班同学,而且在一年级、二年级时还是同桌。后来她们俩虽然不是同桌了,但是仍然是最好的朋友,每天下课几乎形影不离。

阿丽莎平时很文静,说话总是轻声细语。以前班里有个"捣蛋鬼"特别喜欢对她做恶作剧,下课时经常突然跑到她面前,胡言乱语地嚷嚷几声,不等阿丽莎反应过来就跑开了,常常把阿丽莎吓一跳。艾莉知道后找到"捣蛋鬼",警告他如果以后再敢这样做,她就去告诉老师,果然,"捣蛋鬼"再也没敢"打扰"阿丽莎。渐渐地,艾莉成了阿丽莎的主心骨,一遇到什么大事,阿丽莎就找艾莉商量,艾莉也总是大胆地给她一些建议。

六年级的时候，艾莉转了学。转学后，艾莉和阿丽莎几乎每天都会聊聊天，每天都互发信息，有时也视频聊天。艾莉告诉阿丽莎她在新学校里发生的趣事儿，或者讲讲自己新结交的朋友，阿丽莎则告诉艾莉班里的同学尤其是几个"死党"的近况，当然也不会忘记说说班里几个"捣蛋鬼"最近干了些什么奇葩的事儿。总之，两个人总是有说不完的话。不过，不知道为什么，最近艾莉已经连续两周没有阿丽莎的消息了，她发了几次信息，阿丽莎都没有回，艾莉似乎感觉到阿丽莎出了什么事。阿丽莎曾经和艾莉说过，她爸爸妈妈经常吵架，而且很少给她零花钱，她的手机还是前年过生日时奶奶给她买的。

一天下午放学后，艾莉正在做作业，手机铃声突然响了。艾莉丢下手中的笔，飞快地跑去接电话，手机屏幕上出现了阿丽莎可爱的娃娃脸。

"嗨，阿丽莎，怎么这么久没听到你的声音，你快把我忘了吧？"艾莉打趣地问。

"怎么会，我现在在奶奶家。"艾莉明显地感觉到阿丽莎说话的语气有些不对，而且她看上去好像刚刚哭过。

"你怎么了？怎么在奶奶家？学校放假了？现在没什么假期啊！"艾莉一口气问了好几个问题。

"没什么。"阿丽莎边说边低下了头。

不知怎么，电话那头阿丽莎突然哭了起来，艾莉被阿丽莎的举动吓了一跳。艾莉和阿丽莎认识好几年了，偶尔也见过阿丽莎难过的样子,但是从来没见过阿丽莎哭得这么伤心。

"别哭,你到底怎么了?"艾莉急切地问。

"爸爸妈妈吵架,妈妈一气之下撇下我和弟弟去了外婆家,爸爸让我留在家里照顾弟弟,还说以后不让我上学了,由他在家里教我。"阿丽莎边哭边说。

"啊,怎、怎、怎么会这样?"艾莉情急之下结巴起来,"那你自己是怎么想的,你不想上学了?"艾莉疑惑地问道。

"我当然想上学了,而且我给学校老师打了电话,老师也来过了,可是爸爸说他是我的监护人,他有权决定我是否上学,不用老师管。老师后来又来了好几次,可是爸爸就是不同意我去上学,他还把我的手机没收了。今早,趁爸爸不在家,奶奶派人把我和弟弟接走了,所以现在我住在奶奶家。"阿丽莎说道。

"那你接下来怎么办啊?"听了阿丽莎的话,艾莉着急起来。

"我也不知道,我……"阿丽莎说着哭得更厉害了。

艾莉急忙安慰阿丽莎,告诉她别着急,一定能找到解决问题的办法,可是艾莉自己心里也没有底。

挂了电话,艾莉一下午都心绪不宁,无法安心做作业。不知不觉,天黑了。

晚上,艾莉的爸爸下班刚进家门,艾莉就急切地拉住爸爸的手,把事情的经过原原本本、认认真真地给爸爸讲了一遍，生怕漏了一个字。

看着艾莉焦急的眼神，爸爸说道："别着急，你先做作业，过一会儿我们再聊。"

晚饭后，艾莉和爸爸讨论起来。

爸爸：你觉得阿丽莎的爸爸有权不让她上学吗？

艾莉：我觉得没有。

爸爸：好，那我选择和你相反的观点。

我认为，阿丽莎和你一样都是未成年人，她的爸爸和妈妈是她的监护人，对她有监护的权利，有权决定她的事情。父母对孩子的监护权是自由的，不管是学校、老师，还是阿丽莎的奶奶，都无权干涉。

孩子受教育的方式有很多种，可以选择到学校上学，也可以在家里由家长教授，选择什么样的方式让孩子接受教育是父母，也就是监护人的权利。

艾莉：就这些理由吗？

爸爸：是，暂时就这些。

艾莉：我有几个问题想问您。

爸爸：好，请说吧。

艾莉：什么是父母的监护权呢？

爸爸：父母的监护权是父母对未成年的孩子保护、监督和管理的权利。例如：父母有权保护孩子的身体或者财产不受他人的侵害，如果有人伤害了孩子的身体或财产，父母有权追究对方的法律责任；父母有权帮助孩子获得他们应该获得或者可以获得的利益，比如，替孩子决定是否接受他人的捐赠，等等；当然，父母也有权利对孩子的一些行为进行管理和教育，比如，教育和监督孩子不能做一些侵害他人身体或利益的事情，等等。

艾莉：这些事情不能由孩子自己决定吗？

爸爸：因为孩子不论是身体上还是心理上都还未成熟，所以还不能完全保护自己，对一些事情尤其是一些重大的事情还不能独立、全面地思考并很好地做出决定，还需要成年人的帮助。父母是能够帮助孩子的最好人选。

艾莉：法律规定父母监护权的目的是什么呢？

爸爸：当然是为了更好地保护孩子的权益了。

艾莉：虽然是为了保护孩子，但是父母的监护权也不会不受任何限制吧？

爸爸：你觉得呢？

艾莉：我觉得应该有一定的限制，父母也不能想怎么样就怎么样，比如，作为父母也无权随意打骂孩子吧？

爸爸：我同意。父母虽然对孩子有监护的权利，但是也不能滥用这个权利，监护权的行使应该有一定的标准和尺度。

艾莉：那么，父母行使监护权应该以什么为标准呢？

爸爸：应该以是否对孩子有利为标准。换句话说，如果一件事对孩子来说只有权利没有义务，那么父母即使有监护权,也无权替孩子决定放弃这些权利。

艾莉:能举个例子吗?

爸爸:比如,有人无偿给你一笔钱或者你继承了一大笔遗产,只要你不放弃,我和妈妈均无权替你决定放弃。

艾莉:明白了!这些权利是孩子的还是父母的呢?

爸爸:这些权利本来就是属于孩子的,父母只是帮助他们行使,或者帮助孩子管理,或者帮助孩子做决定。

艾莉:如果是这样,我认为阿丽莎的爸爸没有权利不让她上学。

根据我们刚才的讨论,上学是阿丽莎的权利,是阿丽莎自己的事情。上学能让阿丽莎学到更多的知识和本领,让阿丽莎变得更强大,将来不但能更好地保护自己,而且还能找到工作,挣到钱,养活自己和家人。也就是说,上学对阿丽莎有好处,而且阿丽莎自己也想去学校上学,本着对孩子有利的原则,阿丽莎的爸爸应该让她去上学。

爸爸:我同意,让孩子接受教育是父母的义务,父母无权剥夺孩子受教育的权利。

艾莉:这么说,您也觉得阿丽莎爸爸的做法不对了?

爸爸:让我考虑一下。如果阿丽莎的爸爸不让她学习了,这是不对的。但是,如果阿丽莎爸爸让她留在家里由爸爸教阿丽莎学知识,这个似乎可以。

艾莉:那您觉得孩子是到学校学习好呢,还是留在家里由父母教授好?

爸爸：这个我不确定。不过100年前的孩子确实大部分都是在家里学习的，比如，你喜欢看的小说《简·爱》里的简不就是到桑菲尔德庄园做家庭教师，教孩子们读书嘛。

艾莉：那您会把我留在家里由您来教我学习吗？

爸爸：我倒是想，但是不会。

艾莉：为什么？

爸爸：因为我很忙，没时间。另外，我也希望你在学校里认识更多的朋友。

艾莉：我觉得现在的情况和100年前不一样了，现在的孩子到学校读书比在家里学习收获更大。

爸爸：是吗？说说你的理由。

艾莉：学校有严格的作息制度，比如，早晨7:30上课，下午3:30放学。孩子按时上学、按时放学，生活很有规律，长此以往能养成良好的时间管理习惯。

学校能同时开设语文、数学、科学、历史和外语等课程，这些课程通常由不同的老师教授。因此，孩子在学校上学，不但能系统地学习各种知识，还能接触到不同的老师，从他们身上学到不同的东西。人吃五谷杂粮身体才能健康，孩子们接触不同的思想和不同的人才能更全面地成长，否则可能会"偏食"。

另外，学校里有很多同龄的孩子，到学校上学可以交到更多的朋友，参加更多的集体活动。

相反，如果待在家里，即使由父母教授，父母也不一定有那么多专门的时间和精力,系统地教授孩子文化知识。况且,父母一般不可能对语文、数学、科学、历史和外语教学都很有经验。最重要的是,孩子一个人待在家里,没有同龄的玩伴,会很孤单。

爸爸:很精彩,听起来很有说服力!

艾莉:是呀,连您也选择让我到学校接受教育。

爸爸:但是每个家庭的情况不完全一样,父母也有不同的教育理念和计划,况且在家里学习也有它的优点。

艾莉:您觉得在家里接受教育有什么优点?

爸爸:在家里接受教育,孩子和父母在一起的时间会更长,亲子关系会更紧密,孩子被关注的程度也会更高。同时,由于父母更了解自己的孩子,父母可以根据孩子的性格、兴趣、特长、特点,在家里有针对性地、灵活地安排孩子的学习时间和内容,因材施教,更有利于孩子的个性成长。

艾莉:听起来有些道理,但是还是没有说服我。

爸爸:你还有什么不同的意见?

艾莉:我承认,在家里学习,孩子和父母在一起的时间可能会更多,父母对孩子的关注度可能也会更高,但是父母关注度过高反而可能导致孩子的反感或者焦虑。您不是说有时候我不愿意和你们说话嘛,那可能也是因为听你们说得太多了。

另外,现在大多数学校都开设了很多课外活动或者兴趣小组，孩子完全可以在学校里培养自己的兴趣、爱好或者特长。如果孩子或者家长觉得学校开设的课外活动还不够，孩子也可以在课后选择参加校外的活动，以发展自己的个性或特长。

爸爸：也就是说，在家接受教育的优点在学校里都能得到很大的满足？

艾莉：是的，而且在学校上学还有那么多的优点！

爸爸：我觉得你说的有道理，所以我选择让你到学校去上学，没把你留在家里！

艾莉：欧耶！那么法律上是怎么规定的呢？

爸爸：不同国家法律规定得不完全一样，你听说过"义务教育"这个概念吗？

艾莉：以前和阿丽莎一起上学时，学校的课本上就写着"义务教育"几个字，但是我没有仔细想过"义务教育"是什么意思。

爸爸：采取"义务教育"制度的国家的法律规定，孩子在一定阶段，如在高中或者初中之前，有义务接受教育，这个义务既是孩子的义务，也是家长的义务。换句话说，在此阶段，孩子有义务学习，家长有义务让孩子接受教育。

艾莉：这么说，阿丽莎可以回学校上学了？

爸爸：且慢！

艾莉：还有什么问题？

爸爸：虽然大多数国家的法律规定孩子的教育是义务教

育,但是它对教育方式的规定各有不同。有些国家的法律规定,孩子的义务教育是学校义务教育,也就是说,在这些国家,孩子必须到学校接受教育;也有些国家法律规定,孩子的教育虽然是义务教育,但是父母可以自主选择教育的方式。例如,父母可以选择让孩子去学校上学,也可以选择让孩子在家里接受教育。如果父母选择让孩子在家里接受教育,那他们必须获得相关教育主管部门的认可,确认他们已经具备和达到了在家里教育孩子的条件。

艾莉:明白了。也就是说,不管是让孩子到学校读书还是在家里学习,父母都必须让孩子接受教育,这是父母的义务!

爸爸:是的。当然,也有少数国家例外。

艾莉:那我和阿丽莎一起读书的地方实行的是学校义务教育吗?

爸爸:是的。

艾莉:太好了,阿丽莎可以回学校上学了!

爸爸:我有个问题。

艾莉:什么问题?

爸爸:为什么大多数国家的法律都规定孩子必须接受义务教育呢?

艾莉:是为了让孩子们长大以后具备基本的生活能力?

爸爸:完全正确。对于一个国家来说,要保证每个孩子都有机会接受基本的教育,达到基本的教育水平,能满足未来参加工作的基本要求。比如,能识字,能阅读,能进行基础的数学运算,等等。

艾莉:各个国家法律规定的必须接受义务教育的时间会有不同吗?

爸爸:是的,有些国家规定初中及以下是义务教育,有些国家规定高中也是义务教育。

艾莉:那么大学教育会是义务教育吗?

爸爸:你觉得呢?

艾莉:我认为应该不会。因为高中毕业后,孩子已经长大了,他们已经有能力决定自己的未来。他们可以选择上大学,继续接受教育,也可以选择去工作,父母和其他人不能再干涉了。

爸爸:是的。况且,一个社会需要各种技能的人,需要不同教育程度的人,如果大家都上大学了,社会不需要那么多的大学毕业生,让大学毕业生去做高中毕业生或初中毕业生就能胜任的工作,也会造成社会资源的浪费。因此,不是每个人都要上大学,是否上大学完全由个人自己选择和决定。

艾莉:明白了!我现在就给阿丽莎打电话,告诉她我们讨论的结果。

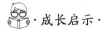·成长启示·

父母虽然是孩子的监护人,对孩子有监护权,但是父母

行使监护权不是无条件的,应该以"对孩子有利"为原则。学习对孩子的成长更有利,所以家长无权剥夺孩子学习的权利,父母应该让孩子接受教育,无论是到学校还是在家里接受教育。

到学校上学和在家里接受教育各有利弊,各国对此有着不同的法律规定。有些国家的法律规定,孩子在一定阶段,如高中或者初中之前,必须到学校上学;有些国家允许孩子在家里接受教育,但是孩子家里必须具备教育孩子的条件,并获得相关教育主管部门的认可。总之,不管选择什么样的教育方式,孩子必须接受教育。

·成长思考·

1. 阿丽莎的爸爸为什么不让她到学校上学?
2. 你觉得在学校上学好还是在家里接受教育好?
3. 你觉得孩子的哪些事情必须征得父母的同意?

Chapter 1

I Want to Go to School!

🦋 Reading Guide

Alyssa's parents got into an argument, and Alyssa's mother left the house to live with her parents. When Alyssa's mother left, rather than letting Alyssa continue going to school, Alyssa's father decided that she should stay at home to take care of her younger brother. Alyssa really wanted to continue her education, and her teachers frequently tried to convince Alyssa's father to allow her to return. Would Alyssa's wish to go back to school come true? Do parents have the right to stop their children from going to school?

Ellie and Alyssa had known each other since first grade; moreover, they were deskmates during first and second grade. Even when they didn't share the same desk during classes anymore, they remained best friends — an inseparable pair.

Throughout her childhood, Alyssa was very shy — her words sometimes even sounded like whispers. When they were little, there was always a troublemaker pulling pranks on her. After every class, he would sneak up behind Alyssa and scream right into her ears. Before Alyssa could even react, he would quickly run off with a smirk on his face. Ellie helped Alyssa stand up for herself by warning the prankster: if he continued to scare Alyssa, she would tell the teacher. This warning was sufficient for the prankster to leave Alyssa in peace. Gradually, Ellie became Alyssa's "other half." Alyssa would come and talk to Ellie when something important came up, and Ellie was always there to offer possible solutions.

After Ellie transferred to another school in sixth grade, the two chatted almost every day. From the daily text messages to occasional FaceTime calls, Ellie told Alyssa about her new school and the new friends she was making. In return, Alyssa told Ellie about what she and their friends were up to, and of course they discussed the jokes that the prankster made! The two of them always seemed to have things to chitchat about. However, for some reason, Ellie had not heard from Alyssa for the last two weeks. Alyssa had not responded to the messages that Ellie sent, nor did she pick up Ellie's calls. Ellie had a gut feeling that something happened to Alyssa. In the past, Alyssa once mentioned that her mother and father often quarreled and that they rarely gave her money to spend. Her mobile phone was given to her by her paternal grandmother on her birthday.

One afternoon, Ellie was doing her homework after school. Suddenly, phone rang with the ringtone assigned to Alyssa's number! Ellie dropped the pen in her hand and ran to accept the FaceTime call. Alyssa's face appeared on the screen.

"Hi, Alyssa! I have not heard from you in such a long time. Did you forget me?" Ellie asked jokingly.

"I would never! I am at my paternal grandmother's house now."

Upon hearing Alyssa's tone, Ellie felt that something was wrong, and it seemed like that Alyssa just stopped crying.

"What's wrong? Why are you at your grandma's house? Are you on break? I don't think there is any holiday recently," Ellie said, asking a bunch of questions in a row.

"Nothing," Alyssa said, lowering her head.

And then, seemingly out of nowhere, Alyssa started sobbing. Ellie was scared and surprised by Alyssa's sudden outbreak. Ellie had known Alyssa for several years, and sometimes Alyssa could be emotional, but Ellie had never seen Alyssa this sad.

"Don't cry! What is going on?" Ellie asked eagerly.

"Mom and Dad got into a fight, and Mom left us to stay at her parents' house. Dad is forcing me to drop out of school to take care of my younger brother. He said that he would teach me at home," Alyssa sobbed.

"Whaaaaaat? How … What … How could he do that to you?" Ellie was so shocked that she started stuttering. "What do you think about this? Do you want to go to school or not?"

"Of course I do! I even called my teachers, and they came to our house and tried to convince Dad to let me go back, but he said that he was my guardian, and he had the right to decide whether or not I go to school. He said that this was none of the teachers' business. The teachers came back to visit again several times, but Dad wouldn't let me go. Then he confiscated my phone — that's why I haven't called you recently. This morning, when Dad was not at home, my paternal grandmother came to pick my brother and me up, so now I am at my grandmother's house."

"What are you going to do next?" Ellie was getting more and more anxious as Alyssa finished telling her what had transpired.

"I don't know, I …" Alyssa said, crying even harder. Ellie hurriedly comforted Alyssa and told her that there must be a solution, even though Ellie had no idea what to do to help Alyssa.

Hanging up the phone, Ellie was uneasy for the entire afternoon, and she could not go on with her homework without thinking about it. As she worried about her friend, the afternoon quickly passed, and the sky darkened.

In the evening, when her father got home from work, Ellie eagerly took her father's hand and told him the entire story, not leaving out any detail.

Looking at Ellie's anxious face, Dad said, "Try not to worry. You should finish your homework first. We will talk when you are finished."

After dinner, Ellie decided to discuss the situation with her father.

Dad: Do you think Alyssa's father has the right to stop her from going to school?

Ellie: I think that Alyssa's father doesn't have the right to do so.

Dad: OK, then I am to argue for the opposite side so that we can understand both perspectives. Because Alyssa is a minor just like you, her parents are her guardians. As her guardian, her father has the right to make decisions regarding her life. Parents have custody of their children, and other people, including the school and Alyssa's grandmother, cannot easily interfere.

Additionally, there are also many ways for a child to receive a proper education. He or she can choose to go to school or stay home to be homeschooled by his or her parents. Parents or guardians have the right to choose which kind of education a child will receive.

Ellie: Are these all of your reasons?

Dad: Yes, these are all for now.

Ellie: I have some questions that I would like to pose.

Dad: Go right ahead!

Ellie: OK, so my first question is: what is guardianship?

Dad: Guardianship, also known as parental custody, is the parents' rights and responsibility to protect, guard, and educate their child. For example, parents have the right to protect the child from any physical harm and property damage. If anyone harms the child's body or property, the parents have the right to hold the other party accountable. They are also responsible for helping the child obtain what he or she deserves to receive. For instance, the parents can decide if the child should receive others' help or donations. Of course, parental custody also includes teaching the child how to act properly and providing a basic education. For example, parents have to educate the children to prevent them from hurting others.

Ellie: Why can't these things be decided by the children themselves?

Dad: Children are not mature enough, both physically and psychologically, and they can't completely protect themselves yet. They don't have the ability to make decisions on certain matters, especially major decisions. They need guidance from adults. Parents are the best choices when it comes to seeking for help from adults.

Ellie: So, what is the purpose of establishing custody?

Dad: It is to make sure that the rights of the children are fully and well protected.

Ellie: Even though it is established to protect the child, the parents' custody over their children should still be limited in some way, correct?

Dad: What do you think?

Ellie: I think that there should be some restrictions. Parents can't do whatever they want to with their children. For example, I don't think parents have the right to beat their child up.

Dad: I agree. Although parents have custody of their children, those rights cannot be abused. There should be certain standards for their actions.

Ellie: In this case, what should be the standards for parental custody?

Dad: It should be based on whether or not an action is beneficial to the child. In other words, if an action brings only rights, without burdens, to a child, then even if the parents have custody of the child, they are not entitled to give up the rights on behalf of the child.

Ellie: Can you give an example of this?

Dad: For example, if someone offers you a large amount of donation or if you inherit a large amount of inheritance, as long as you don't spontaneously give it up, neither your mother nor I have any right to force you to give it up.

Ellie: I understand now! Also, do these rights belong to the child or the parents?

Dad: These rights originally and always belong to the children. Parents are just there to help them to exercise these rights or guide their children to make the right decisions.

Ellie: If so, then I think Alyssa's father has no right to prevent her from going to school.

According to the discussion we had just now, going to school is part of Alyssa's rights, a decision that she should make herself. Going to school can help Alyssa gain more knowledge and skills, thus making her a stronger and more capable person. The knowledge she gains from going to school can be used in protecting herself and making money, and eventually, starting her own family. So, since going to school is beneficial to Alyssa and is something Alyssa wants to do, her father should not prohibit her from attending school.

Dad: I agree that it is the duty of parents to let their children receive an education. Parents have no right to deprive their children of their right to an equal education.

Ellie: So, are you saying that you also disapprove of Alyssa's dad's decisions?

Dad: Let me think about it. If Alyssa's father is stopping her from learning new knowledge entirely, then I disagree with his decisions. However, if Alyssa's father chooses for her to receive education at home, that seems like a legal thing to do.

Ellie: Then, do you think that a child will get a better education if he or she stays at home? Or do you think it is better for the child to go to school?

Dad: I am not sure. However, it was common for children 100 years ago to study at home. For example, in the novel *Jane Eyre* that you like to read, Jane was hired as a governess to educate the child at Thornfield Hall.

Ellie: Then, would you teach me yourself?

Dad: I would love to, but no.

Ellie: Why not?

Dad: Because I am very busy. I don't have time to do that. In addition, I was hoping that sending you to school could help you make friends with who are around your age.

Ellie: I think the current situation is different from that of 100 years ago. Nowadays, children who go to school are more likely to absorb the knowledge than those being homeschooled.

Dad: Is it true? Why?

Ellie: Schools have strict schedules, attending classes at 7:30 in the morning and leaving school at 3:30 in the afternoon. Children go to school and leave school on time. Their study life and routine are very regular. In the long run, they can develop good time management skills.

On top of that, schools also have the ability to set up many different classes and subjects, such as English, math, science, history, foreign languages, etc., which not only helps the students obtain information systematically but also gives students the opportunities to get to know many different teachers and learn about different perspectives. Just like humans have to eat all kinds of nutrients to stay healthy, children also have to be exposed to different ideas and views from different perspectives, or else they could become "picky eaters" and only agree with one idea.

Moreover, there are many children of the same age in the school. Going to school means that you can make more friends and participate in more group activities.

On the contrary, in terms of homeschooling, even if they are well educated, parents are very busy, which means they don't necessarily have enough time and energy to teach children the knowledge that they need to learn. Moreover, many parents might not have the general expertise in English, math, science, history, and foreign languages all at the same time. The most important thing is that if a child stays at home alone without a friend of the same age, he or she would be very lonely.

Dad: That was a good argument! All of those reasons sound very valid and convincing!

Ellie: Thank you! My position is that many people, including you, would choose to send their children to school to receive their education.

Dad: However, you have to consider that every family has a different situation at home and that different parents also have different plans and ideas regarding education. Plus, being homeschooled also has its advantages.

Ellie: What are the advantages?

Dad: I think that studying at home means that the parents could spend more time with the child. That could encourage an emotional bond between the two, and the parents will pay more attention to the child. At the same time, homeschooling means that the parents have increased flexibility when it comes to planning their children's activities and can help a child develop interests in different areas. Having a customized schedule for him or her helps the child to stand out from others and build a more unique personality.

Ellie: These reasons sounded reasonable and intriguing, but they don't convince me.

Dad: Why are you not convinced? Help me understand what you think I'm missing.

Ellie: I agree that being educated at home means that the child can spend more time with his or her parents and that the child will get more attention, but that doesn't always benefit the child. Having all the attention at all times might also stress out the child and subject him or her to more pressure. Sometimes, I act like I do not want to communicate with you, but that's because I think maybe we need a little space from each other.

Nowadays, most schools offer extracurricular activities like sports and clubs after school, which means that the child can still be himself or herself at school and develop interests for a specific field. If that is not enough for the child, then parents can sign the child up for additional activities outside of school.

Dad: So, you are saying that the advantages of studying at home can also be satisfied by sending the child to school?

Ellie: That's exactly it! In my opinion, sending a child to school has considerably more advantages than homeschooling.

Dad: I think you have proved a valid point! That is why I chose to send you to a school instead of homeschooling you!

Ellie: Yay! But what are the laws regarding homeschooling?

Dad: The laws in different countries are not exactly the same. Have you heard of the concept of "compulsory education"?

Ellie: When I attended school with Alyssa, I saw a label on the textbook that says "Compulsory Education," but I haven't thought about the definition of it.

Dad: The countries that adopt compulsory education have laws and regulations stating that children in a certain age range, such as grade school through high school, have the obligations to receive proper education in a school. This is not only the child's responsibility but also the parents' responsibility. In other words, during a certain stage, the children are obligated to learn, and the parents have obligations to allow the children to learn.

Ellie: So, does that mean Alyssa can go back to school?

Dad: Hold up!

Ellie: What other questions do we have to consider?

Dad: Even though most countries have laws stating that all kids must receive education, the rules for receiving education vary. Some countries stipulate that compulsory education must take place in schools. Other countries have regulations stating that even though the children need to receive education, parents can choose to educate their children themselves. For example, parents can choose to send their kids to school or choose to educate their children at home. If parents choose to homeschool their children, they must get the approval from a government agency in charge of education requirements. When they are approved by the agency, it means that they have met the conditions and are allowed to educate their children at home.

Ellie: I understand now. In other words, whether a child goes to school for a systematic education or not, the parents are obligated to provide the child with some type of education because it is their responsibility to do so!

Dad: Yes, however, some countries have different standards.

Ellie: For where Alyssa is attending school, do regulations follow compulsory education?

Dad: Yes.

Ellie: That's amazing! Alyssa can go back to school now!

Dad: Wait one second! I want you to consider one last question.

Ellie: OK. What?

Dad: Why do most countries have laws regulating the compulsory education of children?

Ellie: Is it to ensure that children have the basic ability to live independently when they grow up?

Dad: You got it. For a state, it has to ensure that every child has the chance to receive an equal basic education, where the children become literate and educated to some degree, ensuring that they will have the basic abilities to attend work in the future. Some examples include teaching the kids how to read, write, do basic math calculations, etc.

Ellie: Does the time span for compulsory education differ for each country?

Dad: Yes, some countries define compulsory education as just consisting of middle school education, while others define it as all the way through the end of high school.

Ellie: So, is college education compulsory?

Dad: What do you think?

Ellie: I don't think so. I think that when a child graduates from high school, he or she has already grown up. At this time, he or she can decide his or her own life and future. The child can choose to go to college and continue his or her education, or he or she can choose to work. His or her parents and others can no longer interfere or decide for the child.

Dad: Yes, a society needs people with different skills and educational backgrounds. If everyone chooses to go to college, the society will have too many college graduates, more than what the society needs. We don't want the college graduates to do the work that senior or even junior high school graduates are also capable of doing. That would be a waste of the society's resources. Therefore, not everyone has to attend college, and it should be up to one's personal decision.

Ellie: Great, I will call Alyssa now and tell her that her father has no right to restrict her from going to school!

 Growth Revelation

Although parents are the guardians of and have custody over their children, parents' exercise of guardianship is not unconditional, and it should be based on the principle of "in the best interest of the child." Learning is a way to gain knowledge, something that is beneficial to a child's growth, so parents have no right to deprive a child of the right to learn. Parents should let their children receive education, whether at school or at home.

There are pros and cons of going to school compared to receiving education at home, and countries have different legal regulations regarding this issue. In some countries, children must go to school at a certain stage, such as high school or middle school. Some countries allow children to receive their education at home, but only under the conditions that the child will be educated according to standards set by the government. In short, no matter what kind of education parents choose for their child, the child must receive proper education.

❓ Think and Consider

1. Why didn't Alyssa's father let her go to school?

2. Which do you think is better, studying at school or at home?

3. Do you think children need to ask their parents for consent before making certain decisions or doing certain things? If so, give some examples.

第二章
好心办坏事

·导读·

费利西娅是艾莉在新学校里认识的第一位同学,渐渐地两人成了"无话不说"的好朋友。费利西娅的爸爸给她买了一部 X 款新手机,因体育训练不方便,她委托艾莉帮忙保管,艾莉出于好意答应了,结果贵重的手机却不翼而飞,是谁在捣鬼呢?弄丢了别人的东西要承担赔偿责任吗?

艾莉转到新学校的第一天,教务主任安排费利西娅帮助她熟悉校园,于是,费利西娅成了艾莉在新学校里认识的第一位同学。

费利西娅是学校的"老生",对学校的情况非常熟悉。她几乎能说出每一位同学和老师的爱好和特点,比如,戴尔喜欢旅游,黑尔喜欢科学,黛西家养了一条金毛狗,卡罗尔老师花粉过敏,等等,简直就是个学校"万事通"。

费利西娅家和艾莉家在同一条街上,放学后两人经常一起回家,路上聊聊共同的喜好和开心的事儿,渐渐地成了无话不说的好朋友。

不过,最近情况有了些变化。费利西娅刚刚入选学校中长跑队，每周二和周四下午放学后要留在学校训练，因此，这两天两人不能一起回家，这让艾莉有些遗憾。

周二下午，放学的铃声刚刚响过，艾莉就背着书包冲出了教学楼。远远地，她看见费利西娅正朝着自己使劲地招手，费利西娅已经在操场上准备热身了。艾莉刚跑到费利西娅身旁，费利西娅突然把藏在身后的手伸了出来。

"看，我爸给我买的X款新手机，作为我入选中长跑队的礼物！"费利西娅迫不及待地与好朋友分享自己的快乐。

艾莉对X款手机很熟悉了，因为她哥哥有个同款的手机，她经常蹭着玩手机里的游戏。尽管如此，艾莉还是很新奇地玩赏着好朋友的新宝贝。这时，训练集合的哨声响起。

"艾莉，我要去训练了，带着手机不方便，放在一边又怕丢，你先帮我保管着，带回你家，晚饭后我到你家去取。"

艾莉同意了。费利西娅把手机塞给她就跑开了。艾莉打开背包，把手机丢了进去。

回家的路上要经过一条小河。今天阳光灿烂，河水清澈，要是费利西娅也在，她俩一定会在这儿玩到天黑。艾莉一个人坐在熟悉的大石头上，虽然溪水潺潺、鱼儿跳跃，但她还是觉得无趣，玩了一会儿便起身回家了。

艾莉刚做完作业，读高中的哥哥放学回来了。看到哥哥，艾莉突然想起了费利西娅的手机。

"哥，费利西娅的爸爸给她也买了一款和你那个一样的手机，我给你看看！"说着，艾莉打开背包伸手去摸手机。

可是，她摸了半天也没摸到手机。情急之下，艾莉把背包里的东西都倒了出来，课本、本子、笔摊了一地，唯独没有手机，而且艾莉惊奇地发现，自己背包下面竟然有个洞。艾莉一下子想起来，昨天，家里"可恶"的狗狗一直咬她的背包，她赶了好几次，这个"坏蛋"才恋恋不舍地走开。

"一定是这个家伙干的，看我回头怎么收拾它！"艾莉气愤地想。

可是现在怎么办？费利西娅的新手机丢了，而且还是她爸爸给她买的礼物。

艾莉的哥哥赶紧掏出自己的手机拨打费利西娅的电话号码，可是连续拨了好几遍，得到的回复都是"手机已关机"。

"会不会是手机没电了，或者……"艾莉一下子急了起来。

看到艾莉一脸的焦急，哥哥马上过来安慰她："别急，我们马上原路返回去找，马上，立刻！"

路上，艾莉前前后后、左左右右仔细地查看，不放过任何一个可疑的角落，遇到小树丛也用棍子捅一捅，生怕错过。到了小河边，兄妹俩围着艾莉下午坐过的大石头转了好几圈，可是连个手机的影子也没看见。渐渐地，艾莉的手心已满是汗水。

"再仔细想想，你真的把手机放在书包里了吗？除了这里，你还去过哪儿？"不见手机的踪影，哥哥也有些按捺不住了。

"就放在书包里了,我确定,而且除了这里我没去过其他地方。"艾莉有些委屈。

"那我们去学校看看。"哥哥建议道。

"不会掉在学校的!我在河边的时候还拿出来看过。"艾莉回答说,"不过还是去看看,也许……"

就这样,艾莉和哥哥沿着小路继续找,不知不觉到了学校操场。这时天色渐渐暗了下来,操场上人已不多,费利西娅也早已训练完回家了。尽管艾莉知道手机不会掉在操场上,但她还是和哥哥沿着跑道一圈一圈地寻觅,期盼奇迹出现。然而,最终还是没有发现任何手机的踪影。

回家的路上,艾莉看到行人带着的手机就觉得和费利西娅的手机很像,忍不住多看几眼,弄得哥哥不停地向别人道歉,说对不起。哥哥说艾莉得了妄想症,艾莉也觉得自己快疯了。

渐渐地,艾莉开始有些绝望了,她意识到好朋友的手机被她弄丢了。

"早知道这样我就不帮费利西娅保管了!"艾莉含着泪水说道。

"也不能这么说,你也是好心,况且费利西娅又是你的好朋友,你也不会不帮忙。"哥哥安慰道。

"不过,你不知道自己的书包破了个洞吗?"哥哥继续问道。

"我知道我的书包被狗狗咬坏了,今天我的同学也提醒我说书包坏了,但是我没想到会是这么大个洞,连手机都会漏出去。"艾莉回答说。

"你就是马大哈,粗心的老毛病总是改不掉。"哥哥挖苦道。

"可是我已经改了很多了,你要看到我的进步!而且当时费利西娅急着去训练,我也没想那么多,顺手就把手机放书包里了,我们俩都没注意到书包上的洞。"艾莉辩解道。

"总之,小洞不补、大洞吃苦,你以后做事还是要再细心一点。"听到艾莉说得有些道理,哥哥缓和了一下语气。

"哥,这个手机的价格是多少啊?"艾莉问道。

"差不多600美元吧。"哥哥回答说。

"啊,这么贵!我的零花钱总共还不到100块,全赔也赔不起呀!"艾莉想想都有些害怕。

回到家时,妈妈正在准备晚饭,爸爸还没有回来,艾莉和哥哥赶紧把事情的经过告诉了妈妈。

"别急,孩子们,我先和费利西娅的妈妈说一声,免得她们着急,其他的等你爸爸回来再商量。"妈妈听完后,语气温和地说。

晚上,爸爸下班刚回到家,艾莉就迫不及待地和爸爸聊起来。

艾莉:爸爸,您觉得我有责任吗?费利西娅会不会生我的气呀?我要不要赔偿她呢?要赔多少钱?

爸爸：哦，一口气问了这么多问题！看来，不讨论完这个问题，今天的晚饭你也吃不好。

艾莉：是呀，我很着急！

爸爸：不能着急，着急可能会影响人的判断或决定。

艾莉：这个我知道，我们在排球比赛的时候，如果着急，动作都会变形。

爸爸：平静一些了？

艾莉：嗯。

爸爸：好，我有几个问题想问你。费利西娅为什么让你帮忙保管手机呢？

艾莉：她要参加跑步训练。

爸爸：也就是说她需要帮助？

艾莉：可以这么说。

爸爸：如果你不帮她保管呢？

艾莉：那她会很不方便！您想呀，她总不能拿着手机跑5000米吧？况且还要做些徒手训练。

爸爸：手机很贵重，费利西娅为什么会选择让你帮她保管呢？

艾莉：我们俩是好朋友，她很相信我，她相信我会好好保管，不会弄丢她的手机，可是谁想到……唉！

爸爸：冷静，别急。你明知道手机很贵重，替她保管可能会有风险，为什么还要帮她？

艾莉：她是我的好朋友，她需要帮助，我当然要帮忙了!

爸爸：看来你是做好人好事。

艾莉：对，我纯属帮忙。

爸爸：费利西娅委托你保管手机，你答应了并接过了手机，你们俩之间已经形成了保管合同关系。

艾莉：可是我没有签过字呀？

爸爸：形成合同关系不一定要书面签字，你们的行为已经表明你们之间形成了合同关系。

艾莉：明白了，那么我是保管人了？

爸爸：当然。

艾莉：我有一个问题。

爸爸：什么问题？

艾莉：有一年暑假，我们去奥兰多，返程是晚上的航班。上午退房后，我们把行李寄存在酒店，然后去逛街，傍晚时回酒店取了行李去机场。

爸爸：记得很清楚嘛!

艾莉：环球影城是我的最爱，跟奥兰多有关的事儿我都不会忘!

爸爸：关键是当时你把行李牌弄丢了，服务生翻了半天才找到我们的行李，害得我们险些误了飞机。

艾莉：所以我们当时给了服务生双倍的小费!

爸爸：还罚了你搬行李。

艾莉：唉，往事不堪回首!

爸爸：看来你有丢东西的"前科"。

艾莉：我的问题是，我们和酒店之间是不是也是保管合同关系？

爸爸：当然是。

艾莉：如果当时酒店把我们的行李弄丢了，它是不是应该赔偿？

爸爸：对。如果酒店弄丢了我们的行李，说明它没有尽到保管义务，没有履行好保管合同，应该赔偿我们的损失。

艾莉：那么，是不是不管在什么情况下，酒店弄丢或者弄坏了客户的行李都要承担责任呢？

爸爸：很好的问题！

艾莉：换句话说，在什么情况下酒店可以不承担责任呢？

爸爸：你知道"不可抗力"吗？

艾莉：我知道，您以前提起过，就是像地震呀、洪水呀这些人们无法控制的自然灾害或者事件。

爸爸：对。如果导致客户行李毁损的是这些自然灾害等酒店无法控制的事件，酒店就可以免责。

艾莉：唉，看来我死定了！

爸爸：为什么？

艾莉：狗狗咬坏了我的书包肯定不属于不可抗力，这个我知道。

爸爸：也别那么悲观！再想想看，同样是保管他人的财物,你和酒店有什么不一样?

艾莉:我帮费利西娅保管手机只是为了帮助她,并不是为了赚钱。

爸爸:所以你的保管叫无偿保管。

艾莉:不过,当时酒店好像也没有收取保管费?

爸爸:酒店帮客人保管行李是因为客人在此住店,这是酒店服务的一部分,所以你可以认为,我们支付的住店费用中已经包含了行李保管费,这叫商务保管。

艾莉:明白了。无偿保管之下,保管人就不需要承担法律责任吗?

爸爸:你觉得呢?

艾莉:我觉得,即使是无偿保管,保管人还是有义务保管好财物。

爸爸:可是你并没有收取任何保管费呀?

艾莉:但是我既然答应了费利西娅,就要尽我所能保护好手机,否则以后没人再敢找我帮忙了!

爸爸:很棒,给你点个赞!那么,你要像酒店一样承担责任吗?

艾莉:那样对我也不公平,毕竟我是无偿保管,我只是做好事儿,应该鼓励才对,否则以后我再也不敢做好事了!

爸爸:那怎么办比较好呢?

艾莉:让我想想。

爸爸:好的,不急,给你五分钟。

艾莉：我想好了。

爸爸：说说看。

艾莉：我是无偿帮助费利西娅保管手机，是在做好事，对我的责任要求不能像对酒店要求得那么高，所以，只有在我有重大过失的情况下才承担赔偿责任，这样是不是更好一些？

爸爸：同意，这样对双方都公平。

艾莉：那么在这件事中，我到底有没有重大过失呢？

爸爸：这是问题的关键。

艾莉：这一段我要竖起耳朵听！

爸爸：想想看，手机可能是在哪个环节丢失的？

艾莉：把手机装进书包时我还摸了一下，当时还在，应该没丢在学校。

爸爸：后来呢？

艾莉：后来到了小河边，我忍不住把费利西娅的手机拿出来把玩了一会儿。

爸爸：手机不会掉河里了吧？

艾莉：不会，我记得玩了一会儿后我把手机又放回书包了。

爸爸：再想想？

艾莉：哦！我明白了，狗狗把我的书包外层咬了一个洞，我没留意，可能不小心把手机放在书包外层了。

爸爸：这倒是一个重要的线索！

艾莉：如果我当时在河边不把手机拿出来，或者放的时候留意些，不把它放进外层的口袋里，手机可能就不会丢了。

爸爸：有可能。

艾莉：如果我当时再多留意一下，注意到书包上的洞，我可能会把手机拿在手上或者干脆拒绝帮费利西娅保管手机，那么"悲剧"就不会发生了。

爸爸：这样看来，你似乎是可以做得更好。

艾莉：呜呜，我死定了，看来做好事也要三思。

爸爸：是的，做好事的时候也要看看自己能不能胜任，而且一旦答应了别人，就要认真负责。

艾莉：那可怎么办？这个手机很贵。

爸爸：不要急，虽然"你可以做得更好"，但是我觉得也谈不上你有重大过失。我马上和费利西娅的父母再沟通一下。

艾莉：明白了，我算不上有重大过失，所以我可以不承担责任。不过，我愿意用自己的零花钱承担一部分损失，这样我的教训会深刻一些，就算"交学费"了吧。

爸爸：这个再说，先罚你2个月不准喝碳酸饮料，以根治你马大哈的毛病！

艾莉：好吧。

· 成长启示 ·

商务保管过程中,由于保管不当造成他人财物损失的,保管人要承担赔偿责任。无偿保管是帮助他人的行为,因此,无偿保管人通常只有在有重大过失的情况下,才对被保管财产发生的损失承担全部或者部分赔偿责任。

· 成长思考 ·

1. 费利西娅的手机是如何丢失的?
2. 你觉得无偿帮助朋友保管财物和酒店寄存有什么不同?
3. 如果朋友让你帮忙保管贵重的财物,你会怎么办?

Chapter 2

Good Intention, Bad Outcome

🕮 Reading Guide

Felicia was Ellie's first friend at her new school. The two soon became best friends. Felicia's dad bought her a brand-new iPhone X. Because she had sport practices and could not carry her phone, Felicia entrusted Ellie to look after it. With the intention of helping her friend, Ellie agreed, but she ended up losing it. Who was the "devil in disguise"? Should one be held responsible for losing someone else's property?

On the first day at Ellie's new school, the academic dean appointed Felicia to show her around. Therefore, Felicia was the first classmate that Ellie met at her new school.

As an "old-timer," Felicia was very familiar with the school environment. She could name the hobbies and characteristics of almost every teacher and every student. For instance, Dale liked to travel; Hale was really interested in science; Daisy had a golden retriever; Mr. Carol was allergic to pollen. There were so many more stories to tell!

Felicia lived on the same street as Ellie, so they often walked home together while sharing fun stories. They soon discovered that they shared lots in common, and Felicia and Ellie became best friends.

However, the happy friendship took a sad turn. Felicia made the varsity track team, which meant that she had to stay at school every Tuesday and Thursday afternoon for practices. Therefore, Felicia could no longer walk home with Ellie every day, which made Ellie somewhat melancholy.

On a Tuesday afternoon, right after the school bell rang, Ellie grabbed her backpack and rushed out of the main building. From afar, she saw that Felicia was waving at her to come over to the field where Felicia was warming up before practice. When Ellie came over, Felicia revealed what she was hiding behind her back.

"Look, my dad bought me the newest iPhone X as a present for making the varsity track team!" Felicia could not wait to share her happiness with her friend.

Ellie was already very familiar with the new iPhone X. Her brother had a same one, so she would often sneak onto his phone to play games. Even so, Ellie was still very curious and excited to see her best friend's new "treasure." Then, the coach whistled.

"Ellie, I have to go back to practice, but carrying a phone would be very inconvenient, and I am afraid of losing it if I put it aside. Could you look after my phone? You can bring it home, and I will pick it up after dinner."

Ellie agreed, and Felicia handed Ellie the phone before running off to join the team. Ellie opened the zipper of her backpack and tossed the phone inside.

On her way home, Ellie usually passed by a small stream. The sun was shining above, and the river was so crystal clear. If Felicia was also there, they would definitely hang out there until the late afternoon. Ellie sat alone on the familiar boulder. Although the stream was shimmering and the fish were jumping, she still felt bored. After playing alone for a while, she got up and went home.

Just when Ellie finished her homework, her brother, who was in high school, came back. Looking at her brother, Ellie suddenly remembered Felicia's cell phone.

"Brother, Felicia's father bought her a phone just like yours. I will show you!" Ellie opened the backpack and reached for the phone.

However, she did not feel the phone, even after searching for a long time. In a hurry, Ellie poured out everything from her backpack. Textbooks, books, and pens were everywhere, but no cell phone. As she rummaged through her bag, Ellie was surprised to find that there was a hole under her backpack. All of a sudden, Ellie remembered that she had discovered her puppy chewing on her backpack the other day. It took her a while to shoo the "little devil" away from her backpack.

"It must be this little guy who did this. I have to teach him a lesson!" Ellie thought angrily.

But what should she do now? Felicia's new phone was lost, and more importantly, it was a gift her father bought for her.

Ellie's brother grabbed his phone out of his pocket to dial Felicia's phone number. Even after dialing for a couple of times, the reply was still "the phone has been turned off."

"Maybe the phone ran out of battery, or …" Ellie suddenly got anxious.

Seeing Ellie's anxious face, Ellie's brother immediately came to comfort her, "Don't worry, we will go back and look for it, right now!"

As Ellie and her brother retraced her steps from earlier that afternoon, they looked around carefully. Whenever she saw a suspicious bush, she would poke into it with a branch, just in case. When they reached the bank of the river, the two siblings circled the big stone that Ellie had sat on in the afternoon, but they didn't see a single trace of the phone. Ellie began to panic.

"Let's think about it again. Did you really put the phone in your bag? Did you go anywhere else on your way home?" When they did not find the phone, her brother got a little worried.

"I am sure that I just left it in the bag, and I did not go anywhere else except here," Ellie sounded tearful.

"Then let's go back to school to check," her brother suggested.

"There is no way I left it at school! When I got to the bank of the river, I even took it out to double check," Ellie replied. "But we should still go back. Maybe there's a chance ..."

Ellie and her brother continued to look along the path until they reached the school track field. At this time, the sky had gradually darkened, and there were not many people on the field. The track team, including Felicia, were long gone. Although Ellie knew that the phone was definitely not on the track field, she and her brother still searched along the runway, hoping for a miracle. However, in the end, no trace of the iPhone was found.

On the way home, Ellie could not stop staring at the people who had the same type of phone as Felicia's, resulting in her brother having to apologize to others for her rude behavior. Her brother said that Ellie was getting paranoid, and Ellie agreed that she was getting very concerned.

Gradually, Ellie began to feel desperate. she realized that she had lost her best friend's phone!

"If I knew better, I would not have helped Felicia look after it!" Ellie said, tearfully.

"You can't say that! You are a kind person, and Felicia is also your good friend. You won't say no to helping her," said her brother, trying to comfort her.

"However, didn't you realize that there was a hole in your bag?" her brother asked.

"I know that my bag was bitten by my puppy. Today, one of my classmates told me that my bag had a hole in it, but I didn't expect it to be such a big one! So big that even a phone could fall out," Ellie replied.

"You have to be more careful! Carelessness has always been a problem you struggle with," her brother said, sarcastically.

"But I have changed a lot. You can't ignore the progress I made! When Felicia was eager to join her friends at practice, I didn't think that much. I put the phone in my bag, and neither of us noticed the hole in the bag," Ellie argued.

"In short, if you don't fix a problem when it is small, you will suffer when it enlarges. In the future, you will have to pay more attention to these little things." After listening to Ellie's reasonable explanation, her brother calmed down and eased his tone.

"Hey, about how much is this phone?" Ellie asked.

"Almost 600 dollars," her brother replied.

"What! That's so expensive! I have less than 100 dollars in my bank account, and I can barely afford one-sixth of the phone!" The thought of having to pay 600 dollars scared Ellie.

When they got home, their mother was preparing for dinner. Their father hadn't returned yet. Ellie and her brother quickly told their mother about the incident.

"Don't worry, sweetie. I will first talk to Felicia's mother so that they don't worry. We will fully discuss about the situation when your father gets home," her mother said warmly after listening to Ellie.

When Dad got home from work in the evening, Ellie couldn't wait to discuss with him.

Ellie: Dad, do you think I am responsible for this incident? Will Felicia be mad at me? Do I need to pay her back for the phone? How much should I compensate?

Dad: Wow, that was a lot of questions in a row! Looks like we have to discuss this issue, or else you will not even be able to have dinner peacefully without thinking about it.

Ellie: You're right. I am worried. I want to fix this!

Dad: Try to calm down! When you are nervous or in a hurry, your decision making skills will be negatively affected.

Ellie: I know that. During our volleyball tournament, if we are in a rush to win a point, we often mess up our forms when we are passing or hitting.

Dad: So, are you feeling calmer now?

Ellie: Yes.

Dad: OK. I have a few questions for you. Why did Felicia ask you to look after her phone?

Ellie: She had track practice that she had to attend.

Dad: Therefore, she sought your help?

Ellie: Yes.

Dad: What would happen if you didn't look after her phone for her?

Ellie: Then it would be very inconvenient for her! Imagine if you had to run three miles with your phone in your hand! Plus, she also had to do other stretches and dynamics training.

Dad: A phone is very expensive. Why did Felicia choose to have you look after it?

Ellie: We are great friends, so she trusted that I would take good care of it and not lose it. However, that did not go as planned!

Dad: Calm down, it's okay. Given that you knew that the

phone was very expensive and there were risks that would come with looking after the phone, why did you still choose to help her out?

Ellie: She is one of my best friends, and I want to help her!

Dad: Sounds like you are being a nice person.

Ellie: Correct. All I wanted to do was help.

Dad: Felicia asked you to look after the phone, and when you agreed to do so, the two of you have made an invisible custody contract.

Ellie: But I never signed a contract or agreed to anything directly!

Dad: Forming a contractual relationship does not always require a written signature. Your actions have proved that there is a custody contract between you two.

Ellie: Understood. Then, am I the "custodian"?

Dad: Of course you are!

Ellie: I have another question about being a "custodian."

Dad: What question?

Ellie: When we went to Orlando for summer vacation, I remember that, when returning, we had an evening flight. So, we checked out of our room in the morning and left our baggage at the hotel and went for a walk. When it was time to go to the airport, we came back to pick up our luggage.

Dad: You remember that pretty clearly.

Ellie: Universal Studios was my favorite. I remember everything about that trip!

Dad: If I remember correctly, you lost your luggage tag. The hotel employee had to look around for a long time to find our luggage, which almost made us miss the plane!

Ellie: We also had to tip him a doubled amount!

Dad: And we punished you by asking you to carry the luggage for the day.

Ellie: That was an embarrassing day!

Dad: It seems that you have a "record" of losing things.

Ellie: My question is: was there also a custody contract between us and the hotel?

Dad: Yes, of course.

Ellie: If a hotel loses our luggage, should it compensate us?

Dad: Yes. If a hotel loses our baggage, it means that it has not fulfilled its custody obligations and fails to perform the custody contract. Therefore, the hotel should compensate us for the loss.

Ellie: So, is it the hotel's responsibility for any lost or damaged luggage, regardless of reasons or the circumstances?

Dad: That is a very good question!

Ellie: I guess what I'm asking is: are there any circumstances in which the hotel is not responsible?

Dad: Do you know a term called *force majeure*?

Ellie: I remember you using that term before. It means things like earthquakes, floods, and other natural disasters or events that people can't control.

Dad: Right. If a customer's baggage is damaged by events that are beyond the control of the hotel, such as natural disasters, then the hotel can be exempted from liability.

Ellie: Ugh. I think I am in big trouble.

Dad: Why?

Ellie: The dog biting a hole in my bag is definitely not a *force majeure*. I know that for sure.

Dad: Don't be so pessimistic! Even though both are looking after someone's property, what is the difference between you and a hotel?

Ellie: I helped Felicia to look after the phone just to help her, not to make money.

Dad: So, your custody is called "free custody."

Ellie: However, at the time, the hotel did not charge a custodial fee either, did it?

Dad: Even though it did not directly charge a custodial fee, the hotel was helping guests to look after their luggage because the guests were staying there. This was part of the hotel service, so you can think that the hotel fees we paid already included the baggage storage fee. This is a form of business custody.

Ellie: I understand now. Under free custody, does it mean that the custodian does not need to bear any legal responsibility?

Dad: What do you think?

Ellie: I feel that even if it is free custody, the custodian is still obliged to keep the property safe.

Dad: But you didn't charge any custodial fee, did you?

Ellie: But since I promised Felicia, I have to do my best to protect her cell phone, otherwise she will never ask me for help again!

Dad: That's correct! A big thumbs up to you! So, let's take this one step further: do you have to take as much responsibility as what a hotel would?

Ellie: It's not fair to me. After all, I did not charge her. I'm just doing good things to help others. Therefore, my actions should be encouraged, or else I won't feel motivated to do good things again in the future!

Dad: Then, what should be done instead?

Ellie: Let me think about it.

Dad: OK, no hurry! I will give you five minutes.

Ellie: I am ready.

Dad: Go right ahead.

Ellie: I was helping Felicia to look after her phone for free because I am a kind person. The responsibility I bear should not be as high as the requirements for a hotel. Therefore, I will only be liable for compensation if there was gross negligence. Is that fair?

Dad: Yes, this is fair to both sides.

Ellie: So, in this case, did my behavior constitute gross negligence?

Dad: This is the key to the problem.

Ellie: This is probably the most important part that I have to pay attention to!

Dad: Think about it — where could you possibly have lost her phone?

Ellie: I double checked on the phone when I put it into my backpack. It was still there and could not have been lost at school.

Dad: What happened later?

Ellie: Later, when I arrived at the river bank, I couldn't help but take out her phone and play with it.

Dad: The phone could not have fallen into the river, right?

Ellie: No, I remember that after I finished playing with it, I put the phone back in my bag.

Dad: Is there any other possibility?

Ellie: Oh! I remember now! My puppy bit a hole in the outer layer of my bag. I didn't pay attention to that, so I might have accidentally put the phone in the outer layer of the bag.

Dad: This is an important clue!

Ellie: If I hadn't taken the phone out by the river or if I had paid more attention when I put it back and had not put it in the outmost pocket, I wouldn't have lost it at all!

Dad: That might be true.

Ellie: If I had paid more attention and noticed the hole in my bag, I might have held the phone in my hand or simply refused to help Felicia keep the phone, and then the "tragedy" would not have happened.

Dad: It seems that you could have done better.

Ellie: I am done! It seems that I have to think twice about doing good things.

Dad: Yes, you have to consider whether you can do it well when you agree to do good things, and you must be responsible when you make promises to others.

Ellie: What can I do to fix it? This phone is very expensive.

Dad: Don't worry. Although "you can do better," I don't

think we can say you committed "gross negligence." I will communicate with Felicia's parents right away.

Ellie: I understand. Because there wasn't gross negligence on my part, I don't need to take all the responsibility. However, I am willing to compensate for part of the loss with my own money, so I can learn my lesson more profoundly. It's like a "tuition fee" for the lesson!

Dad: That's for later. First things first, your punishment is that for two months, you are not allowed to drink any sodas. We have to fix your bad habit of losing everything!

Ellie: Ugh! That sounds fair.

Growth Revelation

In the process of business custody, the custodian shall be liable for compensation for the loss of property of others due to his or her improper storage. Free custody is an act of helping others. Therefore, usually only in the case of gross negligence do the unpaid custodian carry full or partial liability for the loss of the property.

Think and Consider

1. How was Felicia's mobile phone lost?
2. What do you think is the difference between helping a

friend to keep property and hotel luggage storage for free?

3. What would you do if a friend asked you to help look after his or her valuable property?

第三章
收留"美少女"

·导读·

艾莉捡到了一只很虚弱的走丢了的金毛犬。在全家人的悉心照料下,金毛恢复了健康并生下了六个狗宝宝,它们成了与艾莉朝夕相处的好伙伴,更成了艾莉家庭的成员。半年之后,狗狗的主人出现了,想要带走金毛和狗宝宝。艾莉能留住这些伙伴吗?捡到的狗狗和它生下的狗宝宝应该归谁所有呢?

艾莉从小就喜欢狗,每次出门,她遇见邻居家的狗狗就迈不动腿,总要停下来,一直玩到不得不离开。由于喜欢狗狗,艾莉特别喜欢阅读关于狗狗的书籍,一本《世界名犬大全》让她对狗狗的种类、习性和血脉如数家珍,什么柯基啊,拉布拉多啊,哈士奇啊,她说起来头头是道。但是很遗憾,艾莉一直没有自己的狗狗,所以她梦想将来有一天自己能开一个大大的狗狗收留院,收留很多很多狗狗。

一天,艾莉放学回家,天色已晚。刚刚走到家门口,她远远地就看见一个毛茸茸的动物趴在家门口的台阶上。乍一看,它好像是一只鹿,因为艾莉家住在树林边,经常有小鹿光顾；仔细再看，艾莉大吃一惊，原来是一只金毛大黄狗。艾莉简直不敢相信自己的眼睛，要知道金毛可是艾莉的最爱。

"嗨！"艾莉小心翼翼地和狗狗打了一声招呼。

金毛抬起了头，一双黑得发亮的大眼睛，长长的睫毛，修长精巧的下颚，两只自然下垂的大耳朵，简直就是一个美少女。艾莉不由自主地捂住了嘴巴，生怕自己的冒昧打扰到了"美少女"。不过，"美少女"似乎并没有那么大的热情，它看了艾莉一眼，便无力地低下头，并发出低沉的呻吟声，似乎很痛苦。艾莉凑近，蹲下，抚摸着"美少女"的头。艾莉意识到，这是一只走丢或者被主人遗弃的狗，可能几天几夜没吃饭，饿得已经没有力气了。艾莉赶紧打开门，用力地把"美少女"拖进屋里。"美少女"好像明白了艾莉的意图，用尽最后一丝力气走到客厅的沙发边上，就一头倒下了。艾莉找了个毯子给它盖上，赶紧给妈妈打电话并叮嘱妈妈顺路买点狗粮。

一个小时后，艾莉妈妈回来了，艾莉急切地向妈妈描述刚才发现金毛的情景。妈妈说这只狗可能是走丢了，长时间没吃东西、没喝水，就病倒了。艾莉赶紧把狗粮打开，"美少女"实在是饿坏了，三口两口就吃完了一大盆狗粮，还喝了满满的两盆水，然后心满意足地睡了。

晚饭后，艾莉和妈妈坐在沙发边，静静地看着熟睡的"美少女"。

"它太美了!"艾莉禁不住地说。

"是很美,不过它累坏了。它的主人一定很着急,明天我问问邻居,看看他们知不知道这是谁家的狗。如果没人知道,我们就到镇上的公告栏里公告一下,看看谁家走丢了狗。"听到妈妈这么说,艾莉心里一沉。

第二天早晨,艾莉起得很早。打开房门,艾莉远远地就看见"美少女"站在楼梯口,摇着尾巴,仰着头,目不转睛地看着她。艾莉不顾穿着睡衣,三步并做两步地冲下了楼,一把抱住了"美少女","美少女"也用头不停地在艾莉身上摩挲,好像在和自己的"主人"问早安。

"看你高兴的,好像是你的狗似的,说不定今天它的主人就把它带走了。"妈妈一边催促艾莉吃早饭一边打趣地说。

听到妈妈的话,艾莉抚摸"美少女"的手一下子停了下来,"美少女"也似乎听懂了妈妈的意思,悄悄地走开了。

放学后艾莉飞奔回家,打开门,果然"美少女"已在门口迎接她了。艾莉丢下书包,冲上楼,"美少女"也跟在她后面冲上楼;艾莉停下来,"美少女"也停下来;艾莉满屋子跑,"美少女"也跟着她满屋跑;艾莉拿着球跑到草地上,将皮球高高抛起,"美少女"突然腾空而起,将球稳稳地叼在嘴里,然后慢慢地跑过来,把球送到艾莉的手里。

"妈妈,它简直太牛了!"艾莉惊呼起来,心里不由佩服起"美少女"来。

就这样,一连几天、几周过去了,"美少女"的主人也没出现。渐渐地,"美少女"成了艾莉的好朋友、好伙伴,更成了艾莉家的一员,大家也很少再提起"美少女"的主人了。

"妈妈,你有没有发现,'美少女'好像比以前'胖'了很多?"一天,艾莉问妈妈。

妈妈莞尔一笑,说道:"是的,它快当妈妈了。"

"什么,怎么可能?"艾莉简直不敢相信自己的耳朵。

"'美少女'刚来的时候就已经怀宝宝了,否则身体也不会那么虚弱。"妈妈回答道。

"那它的房间不够大了?"艾莉忧虑地问。

"是的,所以你爸爸已经把一楼的大房间收拾出来,准备给它和它的宝宝用,以后你每天要多给它加加餐,多带它出去走走。"妈妈叮嘱说。

"好的,没问题!"一想到"美少女"就要升级当妈妈了,艾莉高兴地答应了。

几周后,"美少女"果然生了6个胖嘟嘟可爱的狗宝宝,这下可忙坏了艾莉。艾莉每天都要当队长,组织"美少女"一家7口在草地上做游戏,有时候,几个调皮的狗宝宝还会打架,艾莉就负责拉架,常常顾了东顾不了西。遛狗更是要全家出动,队伍浩浩荡荡,邻居很是羡慕。因为要照顾"美少女"一家,艾莉比以前起得更早、睡得更晚了,不过这样的生活让她很开心。

一天放学回家,艾莉看到家里来了一位叔叔,正坐在沙发上和爸爸妈妈谈着什么。

"这就是我的女儿艾莉,这位是尼克先生,他……"妈妈顿了一下,继续介绍说,"他是'美少女'的主人。"

"你好,艾莉,半年前我带它外出旅行,不小心把它弄丢了。这半年来我一直在寻找,谢谢你把它照顾得这么好,还生了6个宝宝。我知道,你们已经是好朋友了,不过,很抱歉,一周后我要把它们带走了。"尼克先生遗憾地说。

"这不可能,您不能把它们带走!"话还没说完,艾莉马上意识到自己有些不礼貌,眼泪一下子涌了出来。

"我很抱歉,那我先走了。"看到艾莉难过地哭了,尼克先生尴尬地起身告辞。

艾莉冲进房间大哭起来。不知过了多久,天渐渐黑了,艾莉的心情稍稍平复了一些。下楼时,艾莉看见爸爸妈妈坐在沙发上正在等着她。

"'美少女'它们都好吗?"艾莉叹了一口气,问道。

"都好,吃完晚饭都睡了。"妈妈轻声回答道。

"爸爸,我左思右想还是没想明白,想和您聊聊。"艾莉说。

"好的,我已经猜到了。"爸爸回答道。

艾莉:爸爸,您觉得尼克先生有权利带走"美少女"和狗宝宝吗?

爸爸:你的意见呢?

艾莉：我当然觉得"美少女"和狗宝宝是我们的!

爸爸：说说你的理由吧。

艾莉：我的理由很简单。"美少女"是在饥寒交迫，甚至奄奄一息的时候被我们救的，如果我们没有救它，它现在可能已经在天堂了，尼克先生也不可能再见到它。

虽然尼克先生是"美少女"的原主人，可是"美少女"对我们的感情比对尼克先生的感情更深，而且我们也已经把它当成了家庭的一员，因此，如果尼克先生把它带走，可能对"美少女"、狗宝宝和我们一家都会造成感情伤害。

狗宝宝是在我们家出生的，对我们家人和家里的环境更熟悉，我们也更了解每个狗宝宝的习惯，因此，它们更适合在我们家长大。

还有，为了照顾"美少女"和狗宝宝，我们花了很多时间和精力，也花了不少钱。如果就这么让尼克先生把"美少女"和狗宝宝带走了，对我们来说不太公平。

爸爸：不简单的理由！我有几个问题想问你。

艾莉：什么问题？

爸爸：你现在最喜欢的东西是什么？

艾莉：当然是妈妈送我的新手机了。

爸爸：好，那么你希望你的手机被别人偷走吗？

艾莉：当然不希望了！

爸爸：你希望你的手机被别人抢走吗？

艾莉：如果我希望，那我一定是傻了。

爸爸：你希望别人借了你的手机一直不还给你吗？

艾莉：我希望我的手机一刻也不要离开我。

爸爸：如果你的手机真的被偷了、被抢了或者被别人借了不还，你希望法律怎么规定？

艾莉：我希望法官判令他们立即把手机还给我。

爸爸：假如——我是说假如——法律不保护你呢？

艾莉：那我会觉得这样的法律不是好法律，制定这样法律的政府也不是好政府，我们不应该支持这样的政府。

爸爸：所以，法律要保护个人的财产不受任何侵犯，就是我们常常听到的"私有财产神圣不可侵犯"。

艾莉：这是必须的。

爸爸：换句话说，取得财产的方式必须合法，以非法的方式取得财产就会侵犯他人的财产权利，不应受法律保护。

艾莉：所以偷来或者抢来的财产都不受法律保护？

爸爸：当然，不但不受法律保护，法律还要惩罚这些坏人。

艾莉：这下我心里有底了！

爸爸：你的手机是怎么得到的呢？

艾莉：是妈妈作为生日礼物送给我的。

爸爸：所以，它现在属于你所有。

艾莉：这个我确定。

爸爸：可见，赠送是取得财产的一种合法方式。想想看，除此之外，还有什么合法方式可以取得财产呢？

艾莉：嗯，购买！

爸爸：对，你可以到商店里买手机。

艾莉：不过我没钱。

爸爸：别急，面包会有的，一切都会有的！

艾莉：还有什么方式吗？

爸爸：有！我父亲就是你的爷爷去世了，他的一块手表留给了我。

艾莉：我知道，这是继承。

爸爸：继承也是取得财产的一种合法方式。

艾莉：对，《简·爱》里的简就从她死去的叔父那里继承了一大笔遗产。

爸爸：现在我们讨论一下"捡"能不能成为取得财产的合法方式，也就是说，你捡到的东西能不能归你所有？

艾莉：这个我还是不确定！

爸爸：想想看，如果法律规定丢失的东西归捡到的人所有，那么可能会产生什么样的后果呢？

艾莉：我会时时刻刻把手机拿在手上，生怕别人"捡"了我的手机。

爸爸：还可能会出现什么情况？

艾莉：嗯，可能很多人天天在马路上准备捡东西，或者大家都跟在别人的后面捡东西。这太恐怖了吧！

爸爸：所以，法律应该确保一项财产处于稳定的状态。

艾莉：什么叫财产处于稳定的状态？

爸爸：就是使私有财产处于安全的状态，这样手机就不会今天是你的，明天莫名其妙地成为我的，后天又归了妈妈，权属始终处于不确定的状态。

艾莉：如果那样的话，我要天天抱着手机睡觉了。

爸爸：只有财产处于稳定状态，人们才会安心生活，社会才会有序运转。如果丢失的东西归捡到的人所有，那么财产将处于不稳定的状态，所以，"捡"不应该是取得财产的合法方式，这个你同意吗？

艾莉：似乎，好像，嗯……是对的。

爸爸：看来你有点犹豫。

艾莉：不是犹豫，是挣扎！

爸爸："美少女"是我们捡到的，虽然我们很喜欢它，它对我们也很有感情，但是它还是不能归我们所有，它还是尼克的。

艾莉：虽然是这个道理，但是我还是有点不愿意接受。

爸爸：法律就是法律，感情就是感情，感情代替不了法律。

艾莉："美少女"不能归我们所有，那狗宝宝总该归我们所有吧？

爸爸：狗妈妈生了狗宝宝，狗宝宝就是狗妈妈的"孳息"。

艾莉："孳息"是什么意思？

爸爸：孳息就是一项财产产生出的另外一项财产。你还能举出几个类似的例子吗?

艾莉:让我想想,母鸡生蛋?

爸爸:很好,还有呢?

艾莉:枣树结枣?

爸爸:对的。

艾莉:那我是您和妈妈的孳息吗?

爸爸:这个不算。

艾莉:为什么?

爸爸:因为人不是财产。

艾莉:唉,我真想化身为金山银山呀。

爸爸:为什么?

艾莉:这样我明天就不用上学了,您和妈妈就不用上班了。

爸爸:这个我和你妈妈不同意!

艾莉:哈哈,我只是开个玩笑。那钱存在银行产生的利息是不是孳息呢?

爸爸:很棒的问题,给你点个赞!这也是孳息。

艾莉:孳息应该归谁所有呢?

爸爸:似乎应该归主人所有更合理,利息总不能归银行所有吧,母鸡生的蛋总不能归邻居所有吧。

艾莉:我明白了!不过,我们为了照顾"美少女"和狗宝宝确实付出了很多。您看,尼克先生原来只有"美少女",而且"美少女"当时都快要饿死了,但是在我们的照顾下,

"美少女"不仅恢复了健康,还生了6个宝宝,尼克先生真是赚大了!他应该给我们一些补偿,这样才公平,否则以后可能没有人愿意照顾走丢的狗狗或者其他动物了。

爸爸:完全同意!

艾莉:我有一个疑问,农场的饲养员饲养奶牛生了小牛,农场主是否也应该给他一些补偿呢?

爸爸:这个不需要,因为这是饲养员的本职工作,他本身就有照顾奶牛的义务和责任。

艾莉:我明白了。因为我们没有义务或者责任照顾"美少女",我们照顾"美少女"完全是在做好事,所以对于我们花费的时间和金钱,尼克先生应该给予一定的补偿。

爸爸:在没有法定义务的情况下,为了避免他人利益受损而为他人管理财产或提供服务的行为叫作无因管理行为,财产所有人或受益人应该给予无因管理人一定的补偿!

艾莉:很好,这样才公平!我还有个问题。

爸爸:真是"十万个为什么"!说说看。

艾莉:如果是偷了别人的狗并照顾它,把它养大,那么主人需要给予对方一些补偿吗?

爸爸:你觉得呢?

艾莉:我觉得不需要,因为偷盗行为是违法行为,应该给予的是惩罚而不是鼓励。

爸爸:很好!我也有个问题。

艾莉:哈哈,看来我的"十万个为什么"是遗传!

爸爸：如果你捡到的不是一只狗狗，而是一箱苹果，会有什么不同吗？

艾莉：按照刚才的讨论，这箱苹果还是应该归原来的主人所有。

爸爸：那么我们就一直等着主人上门？

艾莉：如果这么做，苹果可能会烂掉，这很浪费！

爸爸：对，这也是财产处于不稳定状态的一种表现。

艾莉：那该怎么办呢？

爸爸：法律规定，捡到的财物仍然归原主人所有，但是，如果超过了一定的时限则归捡到的人所有，以免造成社会财富的浪费。

艾莉：这很合理，我赞成！

爸爸：我有一个好消息和一个坏消息，你想先听哪一个？

艾莉：老规矩，先听好消息。

爸爸：尼克先生打电话过来说，我们帮助他照顾了"美少女"和狗宝宝，而且照顾得很好，所以他愿意给我们一些补偿。同时，他还同意送给你狗宝宝，而且随你挑。

艾莉：耶！坏消息是什么？

爸爸：坏消息就是，尼克先生只愿意给你一只狗宝宝。

艾莉：没问题！我已经喜出望外了！

· 成长启示 ·

法律保护私有财产不受侵犯，因此取得财产的方式必须合法。"捡"不是取得财产的合法方式，所以捡到的财物应该物归原主，但是超过了一定的法定时限，该财物可以归捡到的人所有，以免造成财富浪费。

在没有法定义务和责任的情况下，为了避免他人利益受损而帮助他人管理财产的行为应该受到鼓励，财产所有人应该给予管理人一定的补偿。

· 成长思考 ·

1. 艾莉一家是如何照顾金毛的？
2. 你觉得取得财产的合法方式有哪些？
3. 你觉得捡到的财物怎么处理才公平？

Chapter 3

Adopting "Beauty"

🕮 Reading Guide

Ellie found a weak and lost golden retriever. Under the care of the whole family, the golden retriever recovered quickly and gave birth to six cute puppies. The dog and her puppies became good friends with Ellie and were soon considered part of the family. After half a year, the owner of the dog showed up at their front door and expressed his wish to take his golden retriever and her babies home. Can Ellie prevent her friends from leaving? Who should the dog and the puppies belong to?

Ellie had always loved dogs. Every time that she saw a puppy, Ellie got so excited! She set about to learn as much as she could about dogs, and one of her favorite books was *The Best Breeds of Dogs*. This book helped her learn about different breeds of dogs, their habits and behaviors, their bloodlines and origins, etc. Ellie could identify all kinds of breeds just by looking at them, such as corgis, labradors, huskies, and so many others.

Unfortunately, Ellie did not have her own puppy. Therefore, she dreamed about rescuing more dogs when she's grown up.

One day, when Ellie was walking home from school, she saw a fluffy animal shivering near the doorstep of her house. At first sight, Ellie thought that it was a deer — this would not have been unexpected since Ellie's house was right next to the forest. However, when Ellie took a closer look, she covered her mouth in surprise. It was a golden retriever! Everyone who knew Ellie knew that golden retrievers were her all-time favorite type of dog. She couldn't even believe her own eyes!

"Hey, baby girl!" Ellie ducked and whispered cautiously.

The golden retriever raised her head, her eyes shining brilliantly bright. Her long eye lashes, perfect cheeks and jaw, and naturally flappy ears made her beauty stand out even more than it already did. She was the definition of natural beauty! Ellie could not stop herself from covering her own mouth, in fear of disturbing this beauty. "Beauty," on the other hand, did not seem too passionate about Ellie's arrival. She glanced at Ellie, put her head on her paws, and groaned with pain. As Ellie got closer, she knelt down and gently patted Beauty's head. She realized that Beauty might have been a lost or an abandoned dog that had starved for a few days, and that was why the golden retriever looked so sick. Ellie quickly opened the door and tried to carry Beauty into her house with all her might. Seeming to understand what Ellie was doing, Beauty used her last bits of power to drag herself next to the couches in the living room and laid down quickly. Ellie found a blanket to help make Beauty comfortable. She then went to call her mom to let her know what had happened and asked her to bring some dog food home with her.

An hour later, Ellie's mother came back and was eager to hear Ellie describe the process of finding Beauty. After hearing Ellie's account, her mother said that the dog probably got lost, and because she probably hadn't eaten or drunk anything for a while, Beauty was sick. Ellie quickly filled a huge bowl with the dog food that her mom bought. Beauty gorged all the food down without hesitation; she even drank two cups of water! Seeming satisfied, Beauty yawned with contentment and went to sleep.

After dinner, Ellie and her mother sat by the couch and watched the golden retriever sleep.

"She is beautiful, Mom!" Ellie was so astonished by her beauty.

"I totally agree, but she is super tired. Her owner is probably looking for her right now. Tomorrow, I am going to ask the neighbors if this is their dog. On the other hand, I should probably post about her on the bulletin board in our town, so we can see who lost their dog." When her mom said that, Ellie's heart sank.

On the next day, Ellie woke up very early in the morning. Opening the bedroom door, she saw Beauty wiggling her tail. She was looking up at Ellie. Ellie stormed down the stairs in her pajamas and hugged Beauty as tightly as possible. In return, Beauty licked Ellie, just like how dogs greet their owners.

"Look how happy you are! You are treating her like she is your pet. Maybe the owner is coming today to take her back home," Mom said jokingly as she grabbed breakfast for Ellie.

Ellie was about to pet Beauty when Mom said that, and she suddenly stopped. Beauty seemed to understand what Mom meant, and she snuck away quickly.

After school, Ellie sprinted home. As expected, Beauty was waiting for her when she opened the door. Beauty followed her as Ellie tossed her backpack onto the couch and dashed upstairs. When Ellie stopped, Beauty stopped right behind her. When Ellie got excited and ran around the house like crazy, Beauty did the same without hesitation. After that, Ellie galloped out onto the lawn and threw a baseball in the opposite direction. To her surprise, Beauty jumped high up, caught the ball, and put it back steadily into Ellie's hand.

"Mom, she is amazing!" Ellie exclaimed. She loved Beauty.

As the days and then weeks passed, Beauty's owner never appeared. Gradually, Beauty became one of Ellie's closest companions. After a few weeks, the family stopped mentioning Beauty's owner, and she became part of the family.

"Mom, did you notice that Beauty is gaining more weight?" Ellie asked her mother one day.

"Yes, and that is because she is going to give birth to adorable puppies soon!" Mom chuckled when she saw Ellie's jaw drop.

"What? How is that even possible?" Ellie blinked, not fully believing what she just heard.

"She was pregnant when she first came to our place! That was why she was so weak!" Mom answered.

"Does that mean that her room is not big enough anymore?" Ellie asked worriedly.

"Yes, and that is why your father cleared out the family room on the first floor for Beauty and her babies. Now that you know what is happening, you have to supply Beauty with more food and take her out on more walks!"

"Of course I will! Don't worry about that!" Ellie was filled with joy, and she could not stop thinking about how Beauty was going to be a mother soon!

A few weeks later, Beauty gave birth to six healthy,

chubby puppies. This made Ellie super busy! Acting as a group leader every day, she was responsible for arranging games for Beauty and the puppies! Sometimes the puppies got into little skirmishes, and Ellie always helped to separate and calm them. Whenever the puppies went on a walk, the family had to work together to get all seven of the dogs on the leash. Because she had to take care of the puppies, Ellie had to wake up earlier and sleep later than usual, but she truly enjoyed what she was doing.

One day, when she arrived home from school, Ellie saw that they had a guest who was talking to her parents.

"Hey Ellie! Meet Mr. Nick. Mr. Nick, this is my daughter Ellie. He … umm …" her mom hesitated for a little bit before she carried on, "… is the owner of Beauty."

"Hey there! Nice to meet you, Ellie! Half a year ago, Beauty and I were on vacation together, and apparently, she got lost! I have been looking for her everywhere for the past six months! Thank you so much for taking such great care of her. Her six babies are absolutely adorable. I know that you guys became really good friends, but I am afraid that I'll have to take her away in a week," Mr. Nick said pitifully.

"No way! You can't take them away!" Before even finishing the sentence, tears appeared in Ellie's eyes, despite knowing that what she said was extremely impolite.

"I am really sorry about this. I guess I will come back later ..." Seeing Ellie cry made Mr. Nick feel bad, so he left awkwardly.

Ellie stormed into her room and cried. After a while, the sun started setting and Ellie had calmed down for a bit. When she went downstairs, she saw that her parents were waiting for her in the living room.

"How are Beauty and the six puppies doing?" Ellie sighed and asked.

"They are doing great. They are napping in their beds now, right after they finished dinner," her mother replied quietly and warmly.

"Dad, I am still a little confused about the current situation. Can I talk to you?"

"Yes, and I expected that you would want to talk to me," Dad replied calmly.

Ellie: Dad, do you think Mr. Nick has the right to take Beauty and her puppies away?

Dad: What do you think?

Ellie: I think that Beauty and her babies should belong to us!

Dad: Why do you think that's the case?

Ellie: My reasons are quite simple. Had we not saved Beauty that one evening, she might have been in heaven by now. That means that Mr. Nick would not have been able to see her ever again.

Even though Mr. Nick is Beauty's original owner, Beauty is closer to us now than she is to Mr. Nick. We already consider her as part of our family. Therefore, if Mr. Nick takes Beauty and her puppies away, it might cause harm to Beauty, the puppies, and us emotionally.

The puppies were born at our house, so they are more familiar with our house setting and the environment here. On the other hand, we are more familiar with the needs and habits of each of them, so they are more used to and should continue growing up with us.

Also, in order to take care of Beauty and the puppies, we have spent a lot of time and efforts, not to mention money. If Mr. Nick just takes away Beauty and the puppies, that would be unfair to us.

Dad: These are really compelling reasons! However, I have a few questions for you.

Ellie: What is on your mind?

Dad: What is your favorite item that you have?

Ellie: That would be the new phone that mom gave me.

Dad: OK, so would you want other people to steal your phone away from you?

Ellie: What are you talking about? Of course not!

Dad: Would you want other people to just snatch your phone?

Ellie: It would be abnormal if I said yes!

Dad: Would you want other people to borrow it and never return it to you?

Ellie: I hope it stays with me forever.

Dad: If your phone got stolen, snatched, or taken away, what would you want the judge to do?

Ellie: I would hope that the judge would force them to give my phone back to me immediately.

Dad: What if, and I'm saying what if, the law does not protect you?

Ellie: Then I'll think that the law is not fair and that the government which made the laws is not a good government. I wouldn't support a government like that.

Dad: So that's why the law protects everyone's personal property from any violation. That is why we often hear that "private property is sacred and inviolable."

Ellie: I do agree with that.

Dad: In other words, the way to obtain property must be

legal, and obtaining property in an illegal way would infringe on the property rights of others and should not be protected by law.

Ellie: So, any property that was stolen or robbed from another would not be protected by law?

Dad: Of course not! Not only is such property not protected by law, but the perpetrators should also be severely punished for their actions!

Ellie: I feel safer and more protected now!

Dad: So, how did you get your phone?

Ellie: It was a birthday present from my mother.

Dad: That's right. Therefore, this phone belongs to you.

Ellie: Yes, I am sure of that.

Dad: Therefore, we can see that receiving a gift or donation is a legal way to obtain property. Apart from that, what are some other ways to legally obtain property?

Ellie: You can buy it.

Dad: Correct. You can purchase the phone from a store.

Ellie: But I don't have the money to do that!

Dad: Don't worry, you will earn more in the future!

Ellie: Is there any other legal way to obtain property?

Dad: Yes. When my father, that is your grandfather, passed away, he gave me a watch.

Ellie: I know! This is called inheritance.

Dad: Inheriting is also a legal way to obtain property.

Ellie: Yes, in *Jane Eyre*, Jane inherited a large amount of money from her uncle who passed away.

Dad: Now, let's discuss if finding an object is a legal way to obtain it. In other words, do you think you can keep something that you find on the ground?

Ellie: I am not so sure about that.

Dad: Consider this: if the law regulates that people get to keep whatever they find on the ground, then what can end up happening?

Ellie: I would keep my phone with me 24/7 because I am afraid that someone else is going to pick my phone up and claim it.

Dad: What else might happen?

Ellie: Well, maybe a lot of people are going to pick stuff up from the ground or try to follow you around so that they can pick up the things that you drop accidentally. That sounds really scary!

Dad: It seems that the law should ensure that property is kept in a stable state.

Ellie: What does it mean to keep a property in a stable state?

Dad: It basically means that the property is in a safe position. Now, your phone will forever be yours. It will not become mine tomorrow, nor will it belong to your mother the day after tomorrow. Otherwise, it would be an example where the property is unstable.

Ellie: If my property is not stable, then I will have to keep my phone with me even when I go to sleep.

Dad: People won't live peacefully and the society won't be orderly unless property is stable. If people who find things get to keep them, then property will always be in a state of instability. Therefore, finding objects and picking things up from the ground should not be a legal way to obtain property. Do you agree?

Ellie: Well … That sounds kind of correct.

Dad: You look a little hesitant to agree.

Ellie: It's not hesitation; it is because I am struggling to face and accept the current situation!

Dad: So, in this case, we found Beauty. Even though we love her very dearly and she is also emotionally attached to us, she does not belong to us. She is still Nick's dog.

Ellie: Even though it is true, I still don't want to accept this fact.

Dad: Sometimes the laws are the laws, and feelings are feelings. Emotions can't replace laws completely.

Ellie: Even though Beauty doesn't belong to us, the puppies do belong to us, don't they?

Dad: When a dog gives birth to puppies, the puppies are the dog's *fructus*.

Ellie: What does *fructus* mean?

Dad: *Fructus* is the Latin word for "fruits." It is created when one property produces another. Could you give some other examples of *fructus*?

Ellie: Let me think … A hen and the eggs?

Dad: Great! What else?

Ellie: Jujube trees and jujubes?

Dad: That's also right.

Ellie: Am I considered the *fructus* of you and Mom?

Dad: That does not count.

Ellie: Why not?

Dad: Because human beings are not property.

Ellie: Ah! Sometimes I wish I can become a pile of valuable property!

Dad: Why?

Ellie: Because then I will not have to go to school tomorrow! You and Mom also will not have to go to work tomorrow!

Dad: Well. Your mother and I will not agree to this plan!

Ellie: Ha-ha, I was just joking. So, are interests that we accumulate from a bank account also considered *fructus*?

Dad: That is an amazing point! That is also an example of *fructus*.

Ellie: Who should the *fructus* belong to?

Dad: It seems more reasonable for the *fructus* to belong to the original owner. For instance, interests should not belong to the bank, and the eggs that your hens laid should not belong to your neighbors.

Ellie: I understand now. However, we did spend so much time and efforts taking care of Beauty and her puppies! Look, Nick originally only had Beauty, and she was starving and sick. However, with our care, Beauty is now healthy, and she gave birth to six cute puppies. Therefore, it is only fair to us for Nick to reward us in some way. If he doesn't do that, then no one is going to help other people or animals in need in the future.

Dad: I totally agree.

Ellie: I have a question: if a stockman on a farm helps a cow to give birth to a calf, should the boss, the farm owner, reward him?

Dad: The boss does not have to do so, because this is part of the stockman's job. It is his duty and responsibility to take care of the cow.

Ellie: Oh, now I get it. Because we did not have the obligation to take care of Beauty and only did it out of the kindness of our hearts, regarding the time and money we have spent, Mr. Nick should reward us, thus encouraging people to do good things for the community.

Dad: In the absence of a legal obligation, the act of managing property or providing services for others in their interests is called *negotiorum gestio*, or spontaneous agency, and the owner of the property should give certain rewards or compensation to the manager of the property!

Ellie: That sounds very fair! I still have one more question.

Dad: You do ask a lot of questions — go ahead!

Ellie: If someone steals another person's dog and takes care of it, should the original owner reward or compensate him or her for their "hard work"?

Dad: What do you think?

Ellie: I don't think so. Stealing is illegal; the person should be punished, rather than encouraged.

Dad: That is a great explanation! I have a question, too.

Ellie: Ha-ha, looks like there was a part of our genes that coded for the high tendency to ask questions! We truly are related!

Dad: Say that instead of a puppy, you find a box of apples. Would that make any difference?

Ellie: According to the discussions we had, this box of apples should belong to the original owner.

Dad: Then, does that mean that we should just keep waiting for the original owner to show up?

Ellie: If we do that, the apples may have become rotten before the owner even comes. That would be a waste of fresh apples!

Dad: Yes. So, this is an example of a property in an unstable state.

Ellie: Then, what should we do?

Dad: The law stipulates that a property that is found is still owned by the original owner, but after a certain time limit, it will be owned by the person who has found it so that there would not be any waste of resources.

Ellie: That sounds very reasonable. I agree with it!

Dad: I have good news and bad news. Which one do you want to listen to first?

Ellie: Per usual, good news first.

Dad: Mr. Nick just called and said that because we helped him take good care of Beauty and the puppies, he is willing to reward us. At the same time, he is willing to give you one of the puppies, and you get to choose!

Ellie: Yes! That is so exciting! What is the bad news?

Dad: The bad news is that Mr. Nick is only letting you pick one puppy!

Ellie: That is not a problem! I am beyond excited and grateful!

 Growth Revelation

The law protects private property from infringement, so the way of obtaining property must be legal. Finding and keeping an item is not a legal way of obtaining it. Property found should be returned to the original owner. However, if a certain legal time limit is exceeded, the person who found it can become the owner of the property so that resources would not be wasted.

In the absence of legal obligations and responsibilities, the act of helping others to manage their property should be encouraged, and the property owner should give the manager certain compensations.

Think and Consider

1. How did the Ellie family take care of the golden retriever?

2. What do you think are the legal ways to obtain property?

3. What do you think should happen to the property that you find? Is that a fair decision?

第四章

乐不起来的胜利

·导读·

经过一个赛季的训练和比赛,艾莉和队友迎来了排球年终赛。球队一路过关斩将,闯入了半决赛。半决赛进行得异常激烈,比分交替上升。关键时刻,队友凯莉飞身鱼跃,救起一个几乎不可能救起的球,球队逆转获胜,首次闯入了年终赛总决赛,可是凯莉却在飞身救球时受了重伤!孩子在比赛中受伤,谁应该对此承担责任呢?

小学四年级的时候,因为一个偶然的机会,艾莉走进了排球的世界。最初吸引艾莉眼球的不是排球,而是那个有着一双美丽的大眼睛,脸上总是挂着微笑,永远充满激情和快乐的排球教练埃米莉。艾莉一眼就喜欢上了埃米莉教练,也一下子喜欢上了排球。于是,每周六下午,艾莉的父母都会开车送她去打球,风雨无阻。星期六也成了艾莉每周最盼望的日子,每次排球训练就像一个欢乐的大聚会,带给艾莉很多快乐,更洗去了她一周的疲惫。

六年级时艾莉成功地入选新泽西排球俱乐部,开始了系统的排球训练。正规的排球训练和平时打着玩儿完全不一样，很辛苦，有时甚至很枯燥。教练要求很严，一个动作常常要反反复复练习几百次，甚至上千次。

因为训练，艾莉的腿常常伤得青一块紫一块的，艾莉的妈妈看在眼里疼在心里。

有一次，妈妈忍不住说："艾莉，平时训练不一定要那么拼吧，有些球太危险就不要去救了，比赛时再拼呗。"

"那怎么行！俗话说，台上一分钟，台下十年功。平时不好好练，到了比赛想拼也拼不出来呀！"艾莉振振有词。

功夫不负有心人。经过多年的努力，艾莉卧室的墙上已经挂满了大大小小排球比赛的奖牌。不过，遗憾的是艾莉所在的球队一直没有获得年终赛的奖牌。

今年的排球年终赛在宾夕法尼亚州举行，虽然这不是艾莉第一次到外地参加州际比赛，但是艾莉一家还是全体出动前往观战。

早晨一到体育馆，体育馆里已是人声鼎沸，比赛气氛扑面而来。场馆里放着动感十足的音乐，喇叭里不时传来主持人通报赛程的声音，穿着各式比赛服的队员往来穿梭，纪念品商店里人头攒动，各式美食餐车前更是排起了长队。排球年终赛就像一场欢乐的聚会，难怪队员们这么期待！

9点钟，随着比赛哨声响起，整个体育馆沸腾了。裁判员的哨声、队员的呐喊声、家长的助威声混杂在一起，连近距离的交流也要贴着耳根说话才能听清楚。

上午的比赛波澜不惊，艾莉队赢了两场，输了一场。下午的比赛进行得异常顺利，艾莉队一口气连赢了好几场比赛，队员们虽然有些疲倦但是情绪激昂。

傍晚时分，全队迎来了今天最重要的一场比赛，如果赢下这场比赛，球队将首次闯入年终赛的总决赛。大家心里都憋着一股劲儿，想赢下这场比赛。

比赛开始，队员们进入比赛状态很快，连连得分，比分一路领先。就在大家觉得这局比赛已经没有什么悬念时，队员们突然一下子变得不会打球了，接连失误，而且互相传染，连平时发挥一向稳定的艾莉也出现了发球出界的失误。比分到达20平后，刚刚换上场的莉萨更是出现发球、扣球、接球一连串的失误，一下子输掉了整局比赛，队员们顿时懵了。

局间休息后，队员们的情绪逐渐稳定下来，在场上不停地互相鼓励、互相安慰，奋力地把握每一球、每一分，拼搏和渴望胜利的情绪互相传递，大家终于扳回了一局。

决胜局的比赛更是胶着，双方杀红了眼，都发挥出了较高水平。比分交替上升：5平，10平，15平，20平。关键时刻对方发球下网，比分来到了25：24，艾莉队领先。只要再赢一分，艾莉队便能赢下这场关键的比赛，大家的心都提到了嗓子眼。对方教练叫了暂停，工作人员趁机跑进场地，清理地板上的汗水。

短暂的暂停结束，双方队员重新回到场地，比赛继续进行。这次又轮到莉萨发球，艾莉看了一下后场，此轮凯莉和梅甘都在后场。凯莉是球队的主力自由人，梅甘的一传技术也很好，有她俩在后场，防守有保障。莉萨发球过网，对方一传稳稳垫起，二传起球，主攻高高跃起，"砰"地一记重扣，皮球直奔后场。此时，只见凯莉和莉萨同时飞身跃起扑救，皮球弹起，直奔网口，艾莉下意识地一抹，打了个漂亮的二次球，皮球落地得分。大家似乎还没反应过来，过了一秒钟，全场沸腾了。

艾莉等几名前排队员高举手臂，欢呼着"我们赢了，我们赢了，太棒了，太棒了"跑向了教练。

可是，艾莉突然发现大家的目光都投向了场地中央。原来，刚才救球时凯莉和莉萨用力过猛，两人重重地撞在了一起，莉萨还好，只是腿蹭破了一点皮，凯莉则痛苦地躺在地上，起不来了。队友们赶紧围了过去，俯身给她盖上了毛巾，询问伤势情况。过了一会儿，救护车来了，凯莉被送进了医院。医生诊断说是髋骨骨折，需要马上进行手术。

排球年终赛，一次快乐的排球之旅；一场重要的比赛，经过大家的努力拼搏取得了胜利。队员们本应该很高兴，可是队友受伤了，大家怎么也高兴不起来。

看到艾莉闷闷不乐，晚饭后爸爸主动和她聊了起来。

爸爸：你的情绪不高，怎么了？比赛赢了还不高兴？

艾莉：高兴！毕竟我们球队是第一次闯入年终赛的总决赛，可是一想到凯莉受伤我就难过。

爸爸：我明白。凯莉是你的好朋友，而且她还是你们球队的主力自由人。比赛受伤是常有的事，但是这次她怎么会伤得那么重？

艾莉：比赛打得太久了，我们都很累，而且凯莉基本每一局、每一场都上，比我们更累。

爸爸：人累的时候免疫力和反应能力下降，更容易受伤。

艾莉：我有个问题。俱乐部组织我们参加比赛，这时候俱乐部是我们的监护人吗？

爸爸：很好的问题！

艾莉：我知道，在家里，爸爸妈妈是孩子的监护人。

爸爸：对，这是法律规定的，叫作法定监护，父母想推也推不掉。

艾莉：还有想推掉的？

爸爸：有！有父母遗弃孩子的情况。

艾莉：那孩子到了俱乐部，俱乐部是不是自动成了孩子的监护人？

爸爸：这是不是有点"强人所难"呢？

艾莉：我觉得也是，至少要征得俱乐部同意吧？但是我不确定俱乐部会不会愿意，毕竟监护人的责任很大呀！

爸爸：事实上，孩子也不需要时时刻刻都在监护人的监护之下，比如，你在上学的路上或者你跟朋友一起出去玩，我也没有跟着你。

艾莉：我们也在成长，父母有时候要相信我们孩子！

爸爸：我相信你！但是有时候感觉这也是在冒险。

艾莉：我会努力让您和妈妈更相信我的。

爸爸：如果俱乐部不是孩子的监护人，那么它是不是就没有任何义务了呢？

艾莉：我觉得不应该。

爸爸：为什么？

艾莉：家长把孩子交给了俱乐部，孩子脱离了家长的监护，俱乐部就应该管理好我们的训练和比赛，至少应该保证我们的安全。

爸爸：同意！只有这样，俱乐部才会更有责任心，家长也才会放心地让孩子出去比赛。

艾莉：既然俱乐部负有管理义务，那么是不是发生损害的时候，像这次凯莉受伤，俱乐部就一定要承担责任呢？

爸爸：俱乐部虽然负有管理义务，但是只有在它有过错的情况下，它才承担责任。

艾莉：我明白了！如果俱乐部已经尽了管理义务，该做的都做到了，那么它就不必承担责任。

爸爸：对。

艾莉：凯莉是在飞身救球时与队友碰撞而导致受伤的，俱乐部好像没什么过错。

爸爸：以前听你讲过，凯莉去年受过伤？

艾莉：是的。凯莉去年做过髋关节手术，也是在比赛中摔伤的，不过当时她在另外一个俱乐部。可能就是因为有旧伤，所以她的身体承受不了这么大的比赛强度。

爸爸：这个情况教练知道吗？

艾莉：知道，我们全队的人都知道。但是，这么重要的比赛，教练肯定要派最强的阵容了，所谓"养兵千日，用兵一时"嘛！

爸爸：可是教练也不能仅考虑比赛成绩，而不顾队员的健康呀！

艾莉：那倒也不是！平时训练和比赛时，教练经常会问问凯莉有没有什么不舒服。今天比赛间隙时教练还问凯莉累不累，凯莉说不累。

爸爸：你们教练很细心！

艾莉：而且，凯莉的爸爸也是排球教练，听凯莉说，之前俱乐部就她髋骨手术的事情还仔细和她父母谈过。

爸爸：看来俱乐部已经做了它该做的事情，希望这次纯属意外！

艾莉：凯莉特别喜欢比赛，有时候教练看她累了，想换她下来，她自己根本不愿意！

爸爸：你们这么大的孩子还是经常需要大人的监护啊！

艾莉：呃，我又中计了！

爸爸：我知道，你很想帮助凯莉。

艾莉：是，关键是大家都知道我爸爸是律师。

爸爸：压力有点大！不过还有一个主体，可以看看能不能让它承担一些责任。

艾莉：谁？

爸爸：赛会主办方。

艾莉：哦？

爸爸：赛会主办方应该保证比赛的安全。

艾莉：对的！我觉得，首先它要保证不能让坏人进入比赛场馆。

爸爸：是，有几千人参赛，一定要保证场馆内的安全。

艾莉：所以比赛场馆里有很多保安，人们每次进入比赛场馆都要进行安检。

爸爸：有时感觉有点麻烦，但是为了安全，"麻烦"也是必须的。想想看，赛会主办方还有什么应该做的吗？

艾莉：赛会主办方还要保证比赛场地干净和清洁，因为我们经常倒地救球。

爸爸：也就是说，赛会主办方要保证比赛场地和设施的安全和正常使用。如果是因为场地湿滑导致运动员受伤，赛会主办方就应该承担责任。

艾莉：明白了，所以比赛时工作人员经常进入场地擦地。

爸爸：当时场地湿滑吗？

艾莉：那天打了很多场比赛，大家的汗差不多流干了，而且工作人员擦了好几次，地面不湿滑。

爸爸：看来赛会主办方也没什么过错。

艾莉：唉，凯莉获得赔偿的希望渺茫了！

爸爸：体育比赛，尤其是像马拉松这种长时间的运动项目或者像足球这种身体碰撞激烈的项目，比赛中运动员经常受伤。

艾莉：那我们该怎么办？

爸爸：除了要求赛会主办方或者体育俱乐部加强赛事管理、保证运动员安全外，现在还有一些其他成熟有效的办法来解决这个问题。

艾莉：什么好办法？

爸爸：买保险！

艾莉：对呀，买保险！这样运动员比赛受伤时，保险公司就可以负责补偿。

爸爸：所以，我们经常会听说某个体育明星买了天价保险。

艾莉：唉，可惜我们还不是大明星！

爸爸：不过你放心，我们给你买了运动保险。

艾莉：保费贵吗？

爸爸：不贵，不是天价，但是保额足够了！

艾莉：有个与此无关的小问题。

爸爸：什么问题？

艾莉：运动员受伤治疗可能要花不少钱，那保险公司怎么赚钱呢？

爸爸：不是每个投保的运动员都会受伤啊。

艾莉：噢，我明白了，保险公司是否赚钱主要取决于发生保险事故的概率！

爸爸：对的。

艾莉：不过，尽管我买了保险，我还是希望上帝保佑我不受伤。

爸爸：那是当然！这是我和你妈妈每时每刻的愿望。

艾莉：那凯莉呢？她买保险了吗？

爸爸：应该买了。听你妈妈说，你们俱乐部要求每个队员在进入俱乐部时必须买保险，保险费和学费一起交的。

艾莉：一块石头终于落地了！

爸爸：还没有吧？凯莉还在医院呢。

艾莉：噢，对，希望她早日康复！

·成长启示·

俱乐部虽然不一定是孩子的监护人，但是它有义务管理好孩子们的训练和比赛，保证孩子们的安全，所以，俱乐部应该对孩子在训练或比赛中受伤等损害承担法律责任，但是俱乐部已经尽了管理义务的除外。

体育比赛中运动员经常受伤，所以体育俱乐部和赛会组织者应做好运动员的安全管理。其中，购买保险是保护运动员利益的一个有效措施。

·成长思考·

1. 艾莉是如何喜欢上排球的?
2. 你觉得如何减少或者避免在运动中受伤?
3. 如果你经常参加运动或者比赛,你会买保险吗?

Chapter 4

Sullen Victory

🕮 Reading Guide

After a season of practices and tournaments, Ellie and her teammates were preparing for the final tournament of the season. Putting their best foot forward, the team won a place in the semi-finals. The games were intense and the scores were insanely close. At the crucial moment, Kelly dived to the ground to dig a ball that was almost impossible to save. The team won — they were in the finals! However, when Kelly dove for the ball, she got injured badly! Who should bear the responsibility for an injured player in a tournament?

In fourth grade, Ellie entered the world of volleyball due to an unanticipated opportunity. It wasn't volleyball that first attracted Ellie's attention, but the volleyball coach — Emily. She had a pair of beautiful big eyes, always having a smile on her face and full of passion and happiness. Ellie loved the coach Emily at first glance, and she enjoyed volleyball ever since the beginning. Therefore, every Saturday afternoon, no matter how busy they were or how horrible the weather was, Ellie's parents would always drive her to practice. Saturday became the day that Ellie looked forward most to. Every volleyball practice was a joyous gathering, bringing Ellie a lot of happiness as it helped her push past stress from school.

In sixth grade, Ellie successfully joined the New Jersey Volleyball Academy and began consistent systematic practices, which were completely different from the practices she had when she was playing just for fun. They were intense and sometimes even tedious. The coaches had high, strict standards, and the same drills had to be repeated hundreds of times, even thousands of times.

Because of the training, Ellie often had bruises on her legs, and whenever she was hurt, her mother worried.

Once, her mother couldn't help but said, "Ellie, you don't have to work so hard in daily practices. If some balls seem impossible, just take a break and don't try to dig them. You can do that in the actual tournament!"

"No way! As the proverb goes, 'practice makes perfect.' If I don't put in my full effort during practices, it will be impossible for me to do my best at tournaments," Ellie responded.

Hard work paid off. After years of hard work, Ellie's

bedroom wall is covered with medals from different volleyball games. However, there was one medal missing: a team medal winning the grand finale tournament.

The day of the final came, and Ellie, her team, and many of the parents all traveled to the site of the tournament in Pennsylvania.

The following morning, when the team arrived at the stadium where the tournament was hosted, there were already many other teams there. The atmosphere crackled with tension and everyone was a little nervous. From time to time, the speaker announced schedules for the upcoming games, and different teams in different uniforms rushed to get to their courts. Despite this tension, everyone was happy: the souvenir shop was crowded, and all the snacks and lunch stations had long lines. No wonder the players were all looking forward to it!

At 9 o'clock, as the whistle of the game was blown, the entire stadium was filled with energy. The whistle of the referee, the shouts of the players, and the cheers of the parents all mixed together, making it incredibly difficult to communicate. People had to talk into each other's ears to hear each other clearly.

The team sailed through their morning games, winning two games and losing one. The afternoon matches went very smoothly for Ellie's team — her team won games consecutively.

Although her teammates were tired, they were all very excited.

In the evening, the team faced their most important game of the day. If they could win this game, the team would make it into the finals for the first time this season. Everyone vowed to herself and was determined to win the game.

At the beginning of the game, the players quickly got their heads in the game. As they kept making kills, Ellie's team was winning by a large score difference. Just when everyone felt that there was no doubt that they were going to win this game, the players suddenly began to make small yet fatal mistakes, and the panic affected one another. Even Ellie, who had always been a reliable player, served out of bounds. After the score reached 20-20, Lisa, who just got substituted onto the court, made a series of mistakes in serving, hitting, and passing the ball. All of a sudden, the team lost this set of the game, and all the players were very surprised and confused.

After a small in-between-sets break, the players gradually calmed down. They kept encouraging and comforting each other on the court. They fought hard to keep every ball alive and put in their full effort to earn every point, expressing their strong desire to win. The positive energy was really contagious, and they finally won the second set.

The game of the deciding set was even more nerve

wrecking, and both teams really used all the skills they have got. The score alternated — 5 all, 10 all, 15 all, 20 all. At the crucial moment, the other team missed their serve, and the score reached 25:24, with Ellie's team leading by 1 point. If they could win another point, Ellie's team would then win the entire game. Everyone held their breath, as if breathing would affect how the players on the court played. The coach of the other team called a time-out and the staff took the opportunity to run onto the court to wipe off the sweat on the floor.

After a short break, players from both teams returned to the court, and the game continued. This time, it was Lisa's turn to serve. Ellie looked at the back row setup: in this rotation, Kelly and Megan were in the back row. Kelly was the team's main libero, and Megan was a very consistent passer. They were both in the back for this round, so the quality of the defense was guaranteed. Lisa sent the ball over the net; the other side passed the ball perfectly. The set was high up to the outside hitter; the outside attacker leaped high up into the air. With a loud sound of her hand contacting the ball, the ball went straight down toward the back row defenders. At that very moment, Kelly and Lisa both dived to make a save. The ball was passed high up and went straight toward the net. Ellie subconsciously swung the ball over the net, and it landed perfectly on the ground, right before the libero could reach for it. Time seemed like frozen for a bit. Then, after a couple of seconds, the audience cheered.

As they ran toward their coach, Ellie and several other front row players raised their arms and screamed, "We won, we won! Oh, my goodness! I cannot believe it!".

However, Ellie suddenly realized that everyone's eyes were on the center of the court. It turned out that when Kelly and Lisa were both trying to save the ball, the two slammed into each other. Lisa was fine; she had a small floor burn on her knee. Kelly, on the other hand, was lying on the ground in pain. The teammates huddled around, leaned over, covered her with a towel, and asked about her injury. After a while, the ambulance arrived, and Kelly was taken to the hospital. The doctor diagnosed that it was a hip fracture and Kelly needed surgery immediately.

The end-of-season competition was meant to be a cheerful volleyball trip for all the teams. It was also an important game. After all the hard work and the victory, the players should have been very happy. However, since one of their teammates was injured, no one could cheer the team up.

Seeing Ellie so sullen, Dad took the initiative to talk to her after dinner.

Dad: You seem to be in a bad mood today. What is the matter? Why are you not excited about winning the game?

Ellie: I am extremely excited! After all, it was the first time our team made it into the finals, but it makes me so sad to think that Kelly was injured during the game.

Dad: I understand. Kelly is your good friend, and she is the main libero of your team, too. I know that it is common for players to get injured during tournaments, but how did she get injured so badly?

Ellie: The game took a very long time, and we were all exhausted. Also, Kelly was on for every set of every game, so she was more tired than anyone else.

Dad: When people are tired, their immune system does not function as well, and their responsiveness declines, so they are more likely to get hurt.

Ellie: I have a question. The club organized us to participate in the tournaments. So technically, is the club our "guardian"?

Dad: That is a very good question!

Ellie: I know that at home, parents are the guardians of their children.

Dad: Yes, this is stipulated by law. It is called "legal guardianship," and parents are held responsible for not taking this role.

Ellie: What do you mean? Are you saying that some parents did not want to be the guardians of their children?

Dad: Yes! There have been cases where parents abandon their children.

Ellie: When a child arrives at the club, does the club automatically become the guardian of the child?

Dad: Would that be considered a little too forceful?

Ellie: I think so. We should at least get the club's consent. However, I am not sure if the club is willing to accept that. At the end of the day, a guardian has to bear an immense amount of responsibility!

Dad: Actually, a child does not have to be supervised by his or her guardian at all times. For instance, I don't follow you everywhere when you walk to school or when you hang out with your friends.

Ellie: We are growing too, and parents sometimes have to trust us!

Dad: I do trust you! However, sometimes it feels like we are taking a risk.

Ellie: I will try to make you and my mother trust me more.

Dad: If the club is not the guardian of the child, does that mean the club does not bear any responsibility or obligation?

Ellie: I don't think so.

Dad: Why not?

Ellie: The parents handed over the child to the club. The child is temporarily not under the parents' supervision. The club should be in charge of the training and the tournaments, or at least, it should ensure the child's safety.

Dad: I agree! If clubs are more responsible, parents will feel safe for letting the children play for the club in tournaments.

Ellie: Since the club has a management obligation, is the club responsible for any accident that happens? For instance, when Kelly got hurt today, does the club bear any responsibility?

Dad: Although it has a management obligation, the club only takes responsibility if it is at fault.

Ellie: I understand! If the club has fulfilled its management obligations and has done everything it could, then it does not have to bear the responsibility.

Dad: Right.

Ellie: Kelly dove during the game, which resulted in her colliding with her teammate and caused injuries. It seems that the club did not do anything wrong.

Dad: You told me that Kelly was injured last year, correct?

Ellie: Yes. Kelly also got injured in a game last year and had a hip surgery, but she was at another club at that time. Maybe it was because of her past injuries that her body could not endure the intensity of the game.

Dad: Did the coach know this situation?

Ellie: She did, and so did everyone on our team. However, for such an important game, the coach had to put in the strongest lineup. As the saying goes, a thousand days the country nurtures its soldiers and all for one day's battle.

Dad: But a coach can't only think about the results of a game and neglect the health of the players!

Ellie: That was not the case! When we were training and playing, the coach often asked whether Kelly had any discomfort. During the game today, the coach also asked Kelly whether she was tired, and Kelly said she was not.

Dad: Your coach is very thoughtful!

Ellie: Besides, Kelly's father is also a volleyball coach. According to Kelly, the club talked with her parents about her surgery.

Dad: It seems that the club was doing what it was supposed to do. Maybe it was purely an accident today.

Ellie: Kelly loves to play. Sometimes the coach saw that she was tired and wanted to substitute her out, but she was not willing to do it!

Dad: Looks like kids at your age still need some parental supervision!

Ellie: Hey, I fell into your trap again!

Dad: I know that you really want to help Kelly.

Ellie: Yes, the key is that everyone knows that my father is a lawyer.

Dad: Wow! Looks like the pressure is on me! There is another organization that we could talk about, and it might bear some of the responsibility.

Ellie: Who is it?

Dad: The organizer of the tournament.

Ellie: Really?

Dad: The organizer of the tournament should guarantee the safety of the game.

Ellie: Right! I think, first of all, it must be guaranteed that the no one suspicious is allowed into the stadium.

Dad: Yes, there are thousands of people participating in the tournament, and the organizer must ensure the safety of the venue.

Ellie: So, that was why there were a lot of security guards at the stadium. We were also required to go through a security line to get into the stadium.

Dad: Sometimes it felt a bit troublesome, but for the sake of safety, "trouble" is a must. Let's think, what else should the organizer of the tournament do?

Ellie: The organizer of the competition must also ensure that the courts are clean and tidy, because we often have to dive to save the ball.

Dad: In other words, the organizer of the competition must ensure the safety and the normal use of the courts and facilities. If an athlete is injured because the court is slippery, the organizer should be held responsible.

Ellie: Got it. That's why staff often enter the courts to wipe the floor and ensure that it is clean during timeouts of games.

Dad: Was the court slippery at the time Kelly was injured?

Ellie: Plus, a lot of games took place that day, and toward the end, all my teammates were no longer sweaty. The staff wiped the floor several times to ensure that the ground was not slippery.

Dad: It seems that the organizer of the tournament was not at fault either.

Ellie: It looks like the chance of Kelly getting any compensation is slim!

Dad: In sports, especially in endurance sports like marathon or in sports with highly intense physical contacts like soccer, athletes often get hurt.

Ellie: What should we do?

Dad: In addition to asking the organizers or sports clubs to strengthen their management of events and ensure the safety of athletes, there are also some other mature and effective ways to solve this problem.

Ellie: Like what?

Dad: For example, buying insurance is a good solution!

Ellie: Yes, buying insurance! Then, the insurance company would be responsible for paying any medical bill when the athlete is injured.

Dad: That is why we often hear news about sports stars buying an insanely expensive insurance.

Ellie: Oh, unfortunately, we are not sports stars!

Dad: Don't worry; we still bought sports insurance for you.

Ellie: Is the insurance expensive?

Dad: It is not that expensive; it is bearable, but it suffices!

Ellie: I have a small question that is irrelevant to the discussion.

Dad: What is the question?

Ellie: Medical bills for injured athletes can be really expensive. How can insurance companies make money?

Dad: Not every insured athlete will get hurt.

Ellie: Oh! I understand now! Whether or not an insurance company makes money mainly depends on how many of the insured clients get hurt!

Dad: Correct.

Ellie: But even though I am insured, I still pray that I won't get injured.

Dad: That is for sure! This is also what your mother and I wish for all the time.

Ellie: What about Kelly? Did she buy insurance?

Dad: She probably bought it. According to your mother, your club requires everyone to buy insurance when they enter the club, and the insurance and tuition fees are paid together.

Ellie: That sounds like great news to me!

Dad: Not really! Don't forget — Kelly is still in the hospital.

Ellie: Oh, right! I hope she will recover soon!

Growth Revelation

Although the club is not necessarily the guardian of the children, it is obligated to manage the training and competition of the children and ensure their safety. If it doesn't carry out its obligations properly, then the club should bear legal responsibility for any resulting injury of the children during practices and competitions.

Athletes are often injured in sports competitions, so sports clubs and tournament organizers should take measures to conduct safety management of the athletes. Among them, the purchase of insurance is an effective measure to protect the interests of athletes.

❓ Think and Consider

1. How did Ellie get interested in volleyball?

2. How could you reduce or avoid injury during sports training?

3. If you often participate in sports or competitions, would you purchase insurance?

第五章

狗急跳墙

·导读·

放学回家的路上,看到彼得叔叔家的狗——壮壮独自在院子里,艾莉和贝拉进了院子和它一起玩耍。壮壮是"美少女"的好朋友,也是艾莉的老朋友,但是和贝拉是初次相识,壮壮和贝拉相处得会愉快吗?狗狗咬伤他人,狗狗的主人要承担责任吗?

自从"美少女"离开家以后,艾莉心里空荡荡的,总是觉得家里好像缺了点什么。虽然有一个狗宝宝在身边,但是她还是时常想起和"美少女"在一起的日子,每一件趣事、每一个瞬间都历历在目,就像发生在昨天。

"美少女"在家的时候,特别喜欢和邻居彼得叔叔家的壮壮一起玩。壮壮是一条纯种的德国牧羊犬。它身材颀长,体格健硕,动作敏捷,两个耳朵总是竖着,显得很干练。妈妈说,成年的牧羊犬特别聪明,能够帮助主人看家。

艾莉也特别喜欢壮壮。彼得叔叔出差时常常委托艾莉照看壮壮,艾莉经常带着"美少女"和壮壮一起去散步,因此,壮壮对艾莉的感情也特别深厚。

贝拉是艾莉同年级的同学，两人虽然住在同一个社区，但是不在同一条街，今天放学的时候，她们碰巧遇上，所以一起回家。贝拉没有养过狗狗，不过她也很喜欢动物，于是两人不自觉地聊起关于宠物的话题。

路过彼得叔叔家时，艾莉下意识地往院子里瞟了一眼。

"奇怪，大门怎么没关，难道彼得叔叔今天不上班？"艾莉正在琢磨，突然传来"汪汪"的叫声。

是壮壮！艾莉一下子就听出了壮壮的声音，真是狗未见、声先闻。远远地，艾莉看到壮壮兴高采烈地向她跑过来。艾莉想都没想，拉开大门便迎了上去，两个好朋友紧紧地抱在一起。

艾莉一边抚摸着壮壮的头，一边不停地问："你怎么在这儿？怎么不待在屋子里面？"

壮壮则一个劲儿地用舌头舔着艾莉的脸蛋，逗得艾莉咯咯直笑。

"贝拉，这就是我刚才跟你说起的壮壮，我的好朋友。"看着站在一旁、有些胆怯的贝拉，艾莉赶紧介绍道。

"壮壮，这是我的好朋友贝拉，她也特别喜欢狗狗，来认识一下吧！"

壮壮似乎听懂了艾莉的话，"汪汪"地叫了两声，摇着尾巴友善地和贝拉打招呼。贝拉蹲下身，轻轻地抚摸着壮壮的头。壮壮天生"自来熟"，一头扎进贝拉的怀里，拱来拱去，反倒让紧张的贝拉有些不知所措。

过了一会儿，壮壮突然跑开了。艾莉和贝拉正纳闷，只见壮壮叼着飞盘跑了回来，原来壮壮想玩飞盘了。艾莉接过飞盘，"嗖"地掷出。壮壮"噌"的一声蹿了出去，在空中划了几道美丽的弧线，又一跃而起，稳稳地接住飞盘，然后熟练地原地转身，折返，把飞盘交给了艾莉。整个动作一气呵成，像个训练有素的战士。

贝拉张大了嘴巴，连声惊呼："太棒了，太棒了！"

贝拉也试着用力地把飞盘向草地的远处扔去，壮壮同样快步腾空，稳稳地接住，稳稳地送回，动作干练。贝拉兴奋地跑了起来，壮壮跟着她跑。贝拉一次次地把飞盘扔出，壮壮一次次地把飞盘接回来，送回到贝拉手中。过了一会儿，壮壮喘着粗气跑到艾莉面前，一下子趴在地上，吐着舌头，好像在说："今天的运动量可真大，你不用带我出去遛弯了。"

看到壮壮累得瘫倒在草地上，贝拉得意地说："怎么样，还是不如我吧！"

贝拉边说边一屁股坐在壮壮身边。可能是跑得太急，也可能是太累了，贝拉没有坐稳，整个身子险些歪倒在壮壮身上。突然，贝拉尖叫一声，翻身闪到了一旁，壮壮也趁机站了起来，一瘸一拐地躲到了一边。定神一看，艾莉发现贝拉的腿上有两道深深的牙印，一丝丝的血从牙印里渗出来。原来，贝拉坐下时不小心踩到了壮壮，壮壮本能地咬了贝拉一口。艾莉高声呼喊彼得叔叔过来帮忙，屋里却没人回应。艾莉跑到房门口，发现房门锁着，彼得叔叔根本不在家，但是窗户却开着。没时间想那么多了，艾莉赶紧扶着贝拉回到家，立刻给妈妈打电话，寻求帮助。壮壮则像个犯了错的孩子，安静地躲在墙角，不敢正视艾莉。过了一会儿，门铃响了，彼得叔叔来了。彼得叔叔急切地询问贝拉的伤势，然后开车把贝拉送去了医院。

晚上，爸爸妈妈下班回到家。

妈妈说："接到你的电话后我赶紧给彼得叔叔打了电话，彼得叔叔今天没上班，下午去药店买药，走得急，忘了关窗户，所以壮壮跑了出来。"

吃完晚饭，艾莉马上给贝拉打了电话。电话里，贝拉告诉艾莉不用担心，医生已经检查过了，伤势不算严重，而且还给她用了药，过几天伤口就会愈合，不过，医生还是建议她在家休息几天。尽管贝拉一再安慰艾莉，告诉艾莉这不是她的错，但是艾莉总是觉得过意不去。挂了电话，趁着爸爸不忙，艾莉来到爸爸书房和爸爸聊了起来。

艾莉：爸爸，您觉得彼得叔叔是否要对壮壮咬伤贝拉承担赔偿责任？

爸爸：你觉得呢？

艾莉：我还没想好。

爸爸：我觉得你想好了，只是心里有些矛盾！

艾莉：唉，还是被您看穿了。彼得叔叔是我们的邻居，贝拉是我的同学，手心手背都是肉。

爸爸：抛开个人感情，客观地讲，你觉得彼得叔叔应该对此承担责任吗？

艾莉：我觉得不应该。我和贝拉是自己进了彼得叔叔的院子和壮壮一起玩的，不是彼得叔叔邀请我们去的。彼得叔叔当时不在家，他无法照顾我们，也无法照管壮壮。贝拉受伤是壮壮咬的，不是彼得叔叔造成的，况且壮壮咬贝拉是因为贝拉不小心踩到了它，它是出于动物的本能。所以，我觉得彼得叔叔不应该对此承担责任。

爸爸：有些说服力。你很喜欢狗狗，很多孩子都喜欢养宠物，我们可以先谈谈宠物吗？

艾莉：好主意，这是我喜欢的话题。

爸爸：你觉得人们饲养宠物的主要目的是什么？

艾莉：各种各样，但是主要还是出于喜欢，因为宠物能给人们带来快乐。

爸爸：你们同学家里都有宠物吗？

艾莉：哪有！估计只有不到一半的同学家里有宠物！

爸爸：为什么不是所有的同学家里都养宠物呢？

艾莉：原因也是各种各样。有的是家里没人照顾，有的是不喜欢，有的是对动物皮毛过敏，还有的认为宠物可能会伤人，等等。

爸爸：还有人不喜欢宠物？

艾莉：有啊！有些宠物，喜欢的人把它当成宠物，不喜欢的人可能会认为它是"怪物"，甚至害怕或者讨厌它。

爸爸：看来养宠物不是每个人生活所必需的，纯属于个人爱好。

艾莉：我有个问题。

爸爸：什么问题？

艾莉：宠物是不是个人私有财产？

爸爸：当然是，而且有些宠物价格不菲。

艾莉：是的。以狗狗为例，有些狗狗的售价要几千块甚至上万块，我是买不起。

爸爸：既然是个人私有财产，那么主人是不是有义务管理它呢？

艾莉：对的，我记得之前我们讨论过一个类似的案例。一个家庭主妇在自己家阳台上放了一盆花，有一天大风把花盆刮掉了，碰巧砸到了过路的行人，最后法官判决家庭主妇承担法律责任，赔偿受害者的医疗费。

爸爸：记得很准确！大部分国家的法律都规定，财产所有人有义务妥善管理好自己的财产，因管理个人财产不善造成他人损害的，财产所有人应该承担法律责任。

艾莉：看来彼得叔叔有点悬了！

爸爸：而且，宠物还是一个很特别的财产。

艾莉：对，宠物都有生命，有些宠物还很凶猛。

爸爸：宠物照管不好确实容易影响他人的生活，甚至给他人造成伤害。比如，有些人在公园里遛狗，不及时清理狗的排泄物，路人一不小心就会踩到。

艾莉：呃，这很不道德！

爸爸：不道德的饲养行为还有很多。

艾莉：是。有一次放学，我们几个同学一起回家，看到对面过来一个人，带着两条大狗，走近时才发现它们都没有拴绳。那两条大狗直接向我们扑过来，吓得同学们四处逃散。

爸爸：这是狗主人的不对！

艾莉：我养过狗，有些经验，倒是没怎么害怕，其他的同学脸都吓白了。

爸爸：狗主人没有向你们道歉吗？

艾莉：道歉？您猜他怎么说？他居然说没关系，他的狗不会咬人，只是喜欢开玩笑。

爸爸：这玩笑开得有点大了。

艾莉：是呀！他的狗他了解，别人不了解，自然会害怕的。

爸爸：所以遛狗时一定要把狗牵在手里，免得吓到别人。

艾莉：我的一个同学说，他隔壁邻居家养了很多蛇。

爸爸：蛇！我不喜欢。

艾莉：那个同学的妈妈也很怕蛇，听到这个消息后吓得浑身发抖，晚上都睡不好觉，总梦见隔壁的蛇爬到了他们家里。

爸爸：这真是灾难！

艾莉： 同学的妈妈曾找到邻居，希望邻居不要养蛇了，两家为此还发生了一些争执。

爸爸： 邻居之间应该互相体谅！后来怎么样了？

艾莉： 后来谈妥了，邻居家同意把蛇关在笼子里，保证蛇不会跑出来。另外，邻居还出钱定期在同学家四周撒上驱蛇药，这样即使蛇不小心跑出来，也会远离同学家。听同学说，他妈妈现在晚上能睡好觉了。

爸爸： 看来饲养宠物时，饲养人应该尽到更大的注意和管理义务，以免伤害别人或者影响别人的生活。

艾莉： 同意！

爸爸： 既然养宠物有这么多不好的地方，那么法律是不是应该禁止人们养宠物呢？

艾莉： 我们生物老师好像说过，有些国家的法律确实不允许饲养宠物。

爸爸： 那岂不是剥夺了喜欢宠物的人的自由了吗？

艾莉： 对呀，而且动物是人类的朋友，应该和人类和睦相处。

爸爸： 那你的意见呢？

艾莉： 我觉得不应该限制人们饲养宠物，但是要对宠物的主人提出更严格的要求。

爸爸： 是的。因为很多动物都有危险性，容易伤害到他人，所以很多国家法律规定，饲养的动物造成他人损害的，动物饲养人应该承担法律责任。

艾莉：看来彼得叔叔确定是要承担责任了！

爸爸：别急，也有例外规定，如果损害是由于受害人故意或者重大过失造成的，那么饲养人可以不承担或者减轻法律责任。

艾莉：受害人故意或者重大过失？能举个例子吗？

爸爸：比如，小朋友故意追打动物，激怒了动物，被动物咬伤。再比如，小朋友不听劝诫，擅自喂食动物，不小心被动物咬伤，等等。

艾莉：看来问题的焦点是贝拉有没有故意或者重大过失。

爸爸：是的。

艾莉：贝拉是坐地上时没有控制好自己的身体，不小心踩到了壮壮，肯定不是故意或者重大过失！

爸爸：那我们也来看看彼特叔叔有没有什么管理不当之处吧。彼得叔叔当时不在家，他把壮壮散放在院子里，这有没有什么不妥？

艾莉：我看到不少人家的狗都在自家的院子里玩，以前"美少女"也经常在我们家的院子里玩呀。

爸爸：但是我知道，彼得叔叔平时不在家的时候都是把壮壮锁在屋子里的。

艾莉：是的，今天彼得叔叔出门时忘记了关窗，所以壮壮才跑了出来。

爸爸：彼得叔叔平时为什么这么做？

艾莉：可能是怕壮壮走丢，也可能是担心它跑出去会吓到别人。

爸爸：如果今天壮壮没跑出屋，那么悲剧可能就不会发生。

艾莉：是的，我是看到壮壮在院子里玩儿才进去的。

爸爸：另外，彼得叔叔出去时也没锁上大门。如果大门是锁着的，你们还会进去吗？

艾莉：不好说，但是因为大门没锁，进出确实很方便，所以当时我们没想那么多就进去了。

爸爸：也就是说，如果壮壮不从屋里跑出来，你们就不会进院子里和它玩儿。另外，即使壮壮在院子里面，如果大门锁了，你们可能也不会进去。看来，彼得叔叔还可以做得更好！而且，听你妈妈说，彼得叔叔当时是去医院给壮壮买药。

艾莉：是的，我也听说了。壮壮有一款疫苗没注射，彼得叔叔去药店就是为了买这个疫苗，准备今天给壮壮注射。

爸爸：真是无巧不成书啊！彼得叔叔应该"吃一堑，长一智"，记得以后出门时关好门窗，及时给壮壮接种疫苗。

艾莉：这件事因我而起，我要不要承担法律责任呢？

爸爸：你觉得呢？

艾莉：这个我倒是有点担心。

爸爸：从法律上看，你有没有义务照顾贝拉？

艾莉：应该没有，而且我和她年龄差不多，也照顾不了她什么。

爸爸：同样，从法律上看，你有没有义务监管壮壮？

艾莉：也没有，我不是壮壮的主人，彼得叔叔也没有委托我管理壮壮。

爸爸：所以你应该没有什么法律责任。

艾莉：虽然如此，但是毕竟贝拉是跟着我进入彼得叔叔家的院子的，我还是很内疚。

爸爸：不必内疚了，幸亏伤势不是很重，以后切记，"狗急跳墙"！

艾莉：我明白了。

·成长启示·

宠物作为特殊的个人财产，容易给他人造成不好的影响甚至是损害，所以动物饲养人应该履行严格的注意义务，管理好自己饲养的动物。饲养的动物造成他人损害的，动物饲养人或管理人应当承担法律责任，但是如果损害是因受害人故意或者重大过失造成的，则动物饲养人或管理人可以不承担或者减轻法律责任。

·成长思考·

1. 壮壮为什么咬伤了贝拉？
2. 宠物和其他个人财产相比有什么特别之处？
3. 你觉得饲养动物应该注意些什么？

Chapter 5

A Cornered Beast Will Do Something Desperate

🦮 Reading Guide

On the way home from school, Ellie and Bella saw Strong, Uncle Peter's dog, alone in the backyard. Ellie and Bella walked into the backyard to play with Strong. Strong was good friends with Beauty and an old friend of Ellie's, but it was his first time meeting Bella. Would they get along? If a puppy bites another person, should the owner be held responsible for the puppy's actions?

Even since Beauty went home with her owner, Ellie had felt as if there was a piece missing from her heart, and her household felt odd without Beauty's presence. Although she had a puppy with her, Ellie still often recalled the days when Beauty had been around, and she could recall every story and every moment so vividly as if these events had happened just the day before.

When Beauty was home, she loved playing with their

neighbor Uncle Peter's dog — Strong. Strong was a German shepherd, with a long, muscular body that was extremely agile. His ears were always upright, making him seem smart and vigilant. Mom always said that a grown German shepherd would be extremely smart and would be able to look after his home for his owner.

Ellie enjoyed playing with Strong as well. When Uncle Peter went on business trips, he would often ask Ellie to look after Strong, and Beauty and Strong would take a walk with Ellie together. Therefore, Ellie and Strong quickly became very close friends.

Bella was in the same grade as Ellie, and even though both of them lived in the same town, Bella and Ellie lived on different streets. But today, they ran into each other and decided to walk home together. Bella did not have a dog, but she shared Ellie's love for animals, so the two could not stop talking about pets.

When passing by Uncle Peter's house, Ellie glanced into the yard.

"That's odd. Why isn't the gate closed? Did Uncle Peter not go to work today?" As she was wondering, Ellie heard barking coming from the yard.

It was Strong! Ellie instantly recognized Strong's barking. As such close friends, Ellie didn't have to physically see Strong to recognize his voice. From afar, Ellie saw Strong dashing right toward her. Without thinking, Ellie opened the gate and ran toward Strong. The two friends hugged tightly.

Ellie patted Strong's furry head as she asked, "Why are you here? Weren't you supposed to stay inside of the house?"

Strong continued to lick Ellie's face with his long tongue, which made Ellie laugh.

"Bella, this is Strong, the one I told you about. He is a good friend of mine," Ellie immediately introduced Strong to Bella, who was standing on the side, looking a little scared and hesitant.

"Strong, this is my good friend, Bella. She loves dogs, too. Come here, and say hi!"

Strong seemed to understand what Ellie said, so he barked at Bella with a friendly tone as he wiggled his tail, saying hello to his new friend. Bella knelt down slowly as she gently patted Strong's head. Strong was born an extrovert — he dug his head into Bella's arms, wiggled his body so that he was in a comfortable position. This made Bella, who was already nervous, even more overwhelmed.

After a little while, Strong suddenly ran away. Ellie and Bella were wondering where he was going when he came back with a Frisbee in his mouth. It seemed that Strong was in the mood for a game of Frisbee! Ellie took the Frisbee from Strong.

"Swoosh"! The Frisbee cut through the air and Strong sprinted toward the direction of the flying Frisbee. He leapt high into the air using his back legs and caught the Frisbee nicely with his mouth. When he landed, Strong skillfully turned around, headed back, and handed the Frisbee to Ellie. The entire motion was smooth and steady. He was like a well-trained warrior practicing for battle.

Bella exclaimed, "That is so amazing!"

Bella threw the Frisbee far onto the lawn with all her strength. Like last time, Strong quickly jumped high into the air, caught the Frisbee smoothly, and delivered it back to Bella, safe and sound. Excited, Bella started to run, and Strong followed her everywhere. Every time Bella threw the Frisbee into the air, Strong would fetch the Frisbee and deliver it into Bella's hands. After a while, Strong started to pant breathlessly, so he ran to Ellie, lay on the ground with his tongue out, as if he was saying, "That was a lot of exercising for today! It saved you the trouble of having to walk me today!"

Seeing Strong lying breathlessly on the lawn, Bella smiled proudly, "How was that? Looks like I have better endurance after all!"

As she was talking, Bella sat down next to Strong. Maybe it was because of all the running, or maybe it was because she was tired, Bella accidentally lost her balance, and her entire body started to tilt toward Strong as she was sitting down. Suddenly, Bella screamed in pain as she rolled over to the side. Strong, on the other hand, took the chance to stand up and limped to the other side. Looking closely, Ellie realized that Bella had two deep teeth marks on her legs, and a trace of blood leaking from the marks. What happened was that when Bella sat down, she accidentally stepped on Strong, which led to Strong instinctively biting Bella. Ellie tried to get Uncle Peter to help her, but there was not a single sound coming from Uncle Peter's house. She then ran to the front door, only to realize that it was locked and that no one was home! Ellie quickly walked Bella and Strong to her house and called her mother for help. Strong, like a kid who had made a mistake, hid quietly in the corner of the room, avoiding eye contact with Ellie. Before long, the doorbell rang, and Uncle Peter was at the door. Uncle Peter anxiously asked about Bella's injury and immediately drove Bella to the nearest hospital.

In the evening, Mom and Dad came home from work.

Mom told Ellie, "When I got your call, I immediately called Uncle Peter. Uncle Peter didn't go to work today, but he had to pick up his medicine in the afternoon. He was in a hurry, so he must have forgotten to close the window, which explains how

Strong got out."

After dinner, Ellie immediately called to check on Bella. On the phone, Bella told Ellie not to worry because the doctors had checked on her and said that her wound wasn't very severe. Nurses had applied antibiotics and told her that it would only take a few days for the wound to heal completely. However, the doctors still suggested that she take a few extra days off, just in case. Even though Bella kept comforting Ellie and telling her it was not her fault, Ellie still felt guilty and ashamed of what happened. When she hung up the phone, Ellie ran to Dad's study room and started chatting with him.

Ellie: Dad, do you think Uncle Peter should be held responsible and compensate for Strong accidentally biting Bella?

Dad: What do you think?

Ellie: I am not sure.

Dad: I think you have an answer to it, but you are just hesitant about it!

Ellie: You know me too well! Uncle Peter is our neighbor, but Bella is also my good friend. I don't want to offend either side!

Dad: Without any emotional attachment and from an objective view, do you think Uncle Peter should be held responsible for this situation?

Ellie: I don't think so. Bella and I both took the initiative to go into Uncle Peter's backyard and play with Strong, meaning that Uncle Peter didn't ask us to come over. Uncle Peter wasn't home at that time, so he could not have looked after us or Strong. Bella was injured because of Strong, not because of Uncle Peter; plus, Strong only hurt Bella because she accidentally stepped on him, and he did it out of instinct. Therefore, I don't think Uncle Peter should be held responsible.

Dad: Your reasons sound convincing. You really like dogs, just like many other kids. Let's talk about pets first. How does that sound?

Ellie: That's a good idea! This is my favorite topic!

Dad: Why do you think people have pets?

Ellie: For many reasons, but mostly because they love animals and because animals bring them happiness.

Dad: Do your friends all have pets?

Ellie: Not really! Only about a little less than half of my class have pets.

Dad: Why doesn't every family own a pet?

Ellie: There are all kinds of reasons. For some families, it would be difficult to make sure that everyone could take care of the pet. Others don't like animals as much as we do. Some are allergic to pets, while others think pets might be dangerous and could hurt people. There are so many different reasons!

Dad: There are people who do not like pets?

Ellie: Yes! For some pets, people who like them treat them as pets, but the others who don't might think of them as "monstrous" and may even be scared of or dislike them.

Dad: Looks like having pets is not a necessity for everyone, only a hobby for those who enjoy it.

Ellie: I have a question.

Dad: What is it?

Ellie: Are pets considered property?

Dad: Of course! Some pets are very expensive.

Ellie: Yes! For example, some dogs cost thousands of dollars, or even more! I am too broke to get one myself.

Dad: If pets are personal property, then does a pet owner have the duty to teach the pet how to behave?

Ellie: Yes. I think we have discussed a similar case before. A woman placed a pot of flowers on her balcony. One day, the wind blew the pot of flowers off from the balcony, and it landed right on the head of a pedestrian. After trial, the court held that the woman was legally responsible for the incident and must compensate the pedestrian for all medical expenses.

Dad: That was a very accurate description! According to

most laws, a person has the responsibility to take care of his or her own property. Any damage caused by improper management of property should be compensated by the owner of the property.

Ellie: Sounds like Uncle Peter is in trouble this time!

Dad: Plus, pets are a special kind of property.

Ellie: Yes. Pets are alive, and some pets are very dangerous.

Dad: If pets are not taken care of properly, it might negatively impact other people's lives, or even cause more damage. For example, if someone walks dogs in a park and doesn't clean up after their dogs, then someone else might accidentally step on the excreta.

Ellie: Ew, that is very immoral!

Dad: There are a lot of other examples of owners being immoral.

Ellie: Yes. One time, my classmates and I were walking home from school. On our way home, we saw someone walking toward us with two massive dogs. When we got closer, we realized that neither of them was on leash! The two dogs ran right toward us, which scared both my friends and me, and we had to run away from them!

Dad: That was totally the dog owner's fault!

Ellie: I once had a dog, so I wasn't that scared. My classmates, on the other hand, were sweating because they were so nervous!

Dad: Did the dog owner apologize to you?

Ellie: Apologize? Guess what he told us! He said it was not that big of a deal! His dog wouldn't bite people; they just liked to joke around.

Dad: That was some scary "joking around."

Ellie: Exactly! He knew his dogs very well, but that did not mean that others did as well. It was normal that they got scared.

Dad: So, when anyone is walking his or her dog, the dog must be on a leash so that the dog would not disturb or scare anyone.

Ellie: One of my classmates told me that his neighbor had many snakes as pets.

Dad: Snakes? I don't like snakes.

Ellie: That classmate's mother was also very scared of snakes. After hearing that news, she was shaking! At night, she had a hard time falling asleep because she would always dream about snakes creeping into their house.

Dad: That is awful!

Ellie: The classmate's mother met up with the neighbor and tried to convince them not to keep those snakes in their house. The two families even had some arguments about this situation.

Dad: Neighbors should accept and embrace each other!

What happened afterwards?

Ellie: Eventually, they came to an agreement. The neighbor agreed to lock the snakes up in cages and promised that they would not accidentally sneak out. Moreover, they agreed to pay for snake repellents to be used around the neighborhood. Therefore, even if the snakes accidentally sneak out, they will still stay away from other people's houses. According to my classmate, his mom can go to sleep feeling safe now.

Dad: Looks like having a pet means that the owner must pay more attention and take steps to make sure that the pet will not hurt others.

Ellie: I agree!

Dad: Since there are so many cons to having pets, shouldn't the law prohibit people from owning pets?

Ellie: Our biology teacher once told us that some countries do prohibit people from having pets.

Dad: Doesn't that take away the fun for many pet lovers?

Ellie: Yes! Moreover, animals are our friends, so we should all coexist peacefully.

Dad: What's your opinion?

Ellie: I don't think people should be prohibited from have pets, but instead, the government should set strict rules for pet owners.

Dad: Yes. Because a lot of pets can be dangerous and hurt others, many countries have regulations stating that if a pet has caused harm to others, then the owner of the pet should bear all legal responsibility.

Ellie: It looks like Uncle Peter will be held responsible for sure!

Dad: Not so fast. There are still exceptions. If the harm was caused on purpose by the victim or the victim acted in gross negligence, then the owner should bear minimal to no legal responsibility.

Ellie: On purpose or act in gross negligence? Can you give an example?

Dad: For example, some children might chase and hurt a pet on purpose and end up being harmed by the pet. Another example would be feeding an animal when warned not to and thus being bitten by it.

Ellie: It looks like the focus of the question is whether or not Bella provoked Strong on purpose or exhibited gross negligence.

Dad: Yes.

Ellie: When Bella was sitting down, she did not control her body motions, stepping on Strong accidentally. It definitely was not on purpose, and nor was it gross negligence!

Dad: Then let's take a look at whether or not Uncle Peter has done anything wrong in fulfilling his management obligations. Uncle Peter wasn't home at the time, and Strong was left in the yard. Was that appropriate?

Ellie: I have seen many dogs in our neighborhood playing in the backyards. Beauty also used to run around in our backyard.

Dad: I know that, but Uncle Peter usually locks Strong in his room when he leaves the house.

Ellie: Exactly, but Uncle Peter forgot to close the window when he left the house today. That's how Strong sneaked outside the house.

Dad: Why would Uncle Peter usually lock Strong in his own room?

Ellie: Maybe it's because he is afraid that Strong might wander off and get lost, or maybe it's because he is worried that Strong would run outside and scare someone.

Dad: If Strong didn't sneak out of the house today, then the tragedy might not have happened.

Ellie: Yes, I went into the backyard only because I saw Strong running around.

Dad: In addition, Uncle Peter did not lock the gate of the backyard when he went out. If the gate was locked, would you still go in?

Ellie: It's hard to say, but it was very convenient to enter the backyard when the gate was unlocked, so we didn't think too much about it at that time.

Dad: In other words, if Strong had not sneaked out of the house, you wouldn't have entered the backyard to play with him. In addition, even if you saw Strong in the yard, if the gate had been locked, you might not have entered. It seems that Uncle Peter could have done better! Plus, according to your mother, Uncle Peter was going to the veterinarian to buy medicine for Strong.

Ellie: Yes, I heard about it, too. Strong had to get vaccinated for something. Uncle Peter went to the veterinary to buy the vaccine and was planning to give Strong the shot today.

Dad: That was so coincidental! Uncle Peter should learn from his mistakes to remember to close the doors and windows when going out and to vaccinate Strong in time.

Ellie: This whole incident happened because of me. Do I need to bear any legal responsibility?

Dad: What do you think?

Ellie: I am a little scared for the answer.

Dad: From a legal point of view, do you have the obligation to take care of Bella?

Ellie: I shouldn't bear such responsibility, since I am about the same age as her and can't take care of her.

Dad: Again, from a legal perspective, are you obligated to supervise Strong?

Ellie: No, I am not the owner of Strong, and nor did Uncle Peter entrust me to look after Strong.

Dad: Then, you should not be obligated to bear any legal responsibility.

Ellie: Even so, after all, Bella followed me into the yard of Uncle Peter's house. I still feel a little guilty.

Dad: You don't have to feel guilty. Fortunately, the injury is not very severe. Remember, a cornered beast will do something desperate!

Ellie: I understand.

 Growth Revelation

As a special kind of personal property, pets might disturb or even harm others. Therefore, animal owners or caretakers should fulfill a strict duty of care and manage their own animals carefully. Animal owners should be held liable for any injury or damage caused by the animal. However, if the damage was caused by the victim on purpose or if the victim acted in gross negligence, then the owner of the pet will bear minimal or no legal responsibility for the injury.

Think and Consider

1. Why did Strong bite Bella?

2. What is special about pets compared with other personal assets?

3. What are the things that need special attention when it comes to taking care of animals?

第六章
紧急避险

·导读·

艾莉在游泳馆里游泳,碰到"大块头"欧文游泳溺水,热心的利奥飞身入池营救。欧文拼命挣扎,情急之下,利奥打晕了欧文。欧文能获救吗?救人之后,利奥心情为什么不好?水中救人,情急之下,采取一些紧急措施导致落水者受伤,施救者要承担法律责任吗?

艾莉很喜欢游泳而且成绩不错,五年级时,她还曾入选校游泳队。转学后,她虽然没有在新学校的校游泳队继续训练,但是还是经常到她家附近的游泳馆,坚持练习游泳。

这天放学后,艾莉一个人去游泳馆游泳。可能因为不是周末的缘故,游泳馆里的人不多,平时几个要好的伙伴也都没有来。艾莉远远地看见了利奥,利奥是游泳馆的常客,几乎每天都来游泳。按照他自己的说法,他自出生起就开始在这个游泳馆里游泳,游了快二十年了。

利奥不但游泳技术好,而且还"好为人师"。不忙的时候,他经常给大家指导指导,帮助大家纠正纠正动作。他还经常提醒大家,水里的温度通常低于陆地上的温度,长时间在水中游泳，尤其是在江河湖海中游泳，肌肉容易僵硬，可能会导致脚部或腿部抽筋。如果脚部或者腿部抽筋，千万不能着急，要保持冷静，深吸一口气，潜入水中使身体漂浮起来，用手抓住自己的脚尖，用力往自身方向拉伸，重复多做几次，然后争取尽快上岸休息。看来，利奥真该当一名游泳教练！

"嗨，艾莉，今天三道是特意留给你的！"利奥总是大着嗓门，热情地和每一个人打招呼。

"三"是艾莉最喜欢的数字，三道也是艾莉和利奥都喜欢的道次。

"谢谢你的好意，希望周末你还能给我留着三道。"艾莉同样大着嗓门打趣道。

"不过你不会寂寞，欧文今天在第四道。"利奥挤着眼睛补充道。

这时艾莉才注意到第四道水花阵阵，欧文正在"吃力"地游着。

欧文身高188厘米左右，体重将近95千克，着实是个"大块头"。他刚刚学会游泳，劲头儿正足。教练说过，欧文脑瓜很聪明，但可能因为以前运动得不多，所以他身体协调性不是太好，游泳时肌肉紧张，不过他最近进步得很快。

热身后，艾莉跃身入池，熟练地游了起来。今天水温稍微有点冷，不过这正是艾莉喜欢的温度。触壁、转身、再触壁，几个来回下来，艾莉感觉身体微微发热，看来身体差不多舒展开了。透光余光，艾莉看到欧文离自己大概有半个泳池的距离。

"今天感觉不错，可以多练一会。"艾莉在心里暗暗地想。

一个来回结束，艾莉刚刚触壁，准备转身，忽然听到远处传来呼救声。艾莉下意识地急刹车，单手扶壁停住，扭头望过去。只见远处水池中央溅起了巨大的水花，欧文正拼命地拍打水面并发出呼噜呼噜的叫喊声："救命，救命！"

"是欧文，他溺水了！"多年的游泳经验让艾莉第一时间做出了判断。

她刚缓过神，起身准备去营救，一个熟悉的身影已飞身入池。是利奥！只见他飞快地游到欧文背后，从后面一下子搂住了欧文的脖子，瞬间，欧文停止了呼叫，游泳馆恢复了刚才的平静，两人缓慢地向岸边挪动……突然，水面上水花又起，似乎是欧文和利奥扭打在一起。不过，欧文很快又恢复了平静，好像睡着了。此时，艾莉已飞快地赶到，与利奥一起拖着欧文向岸边游去。艾莉以前听别人讲过，人溺水后会变得很重，但是没想到会这么重！岸边的几个人马上围过来，大家七手八脚，一通儿忙碌，总算把欧文拖上了岸。欧文脸色煞白，不省人事，利奥赶紧给他做人工呼吸。过了一会儿，欧文醒了过来，这时急救车也赶到了，欧文被送进了医院。送走欧文后，大家才缓过神，忙问利奥刚才发生了什么事。

利奥说:"我从背后抱住欧文后,刚开始还好,但欧文手臂很长,他突然反手抓住我的手臂,拼命地往下拉,弄得我没法施救。于是,我打了他头部一拳,欧文晕了过去,这样我才把他拖上岸。说起来真是后怕,游泳这么多年,这种情况我还是第一次遇到。"说完,利奥沉默了。

过了几天,艾莉又去了游泳馆,但没有见到利奥。游泳馆管理员告诉艾莉,利奥这几天心情不好,因为上次救欧文时他那一拳打得太重,导致欧文脑震荡。虽然不会有什么生命危险,但欧文需要住院治疗,估计要花不少医疗费。

艾莉担心起来,回到家里便和爸爸聊起这件事。

艾莉:爸爸,您觉得利奥应该承担法律责任吗?

爸爸:我认为应该承担。欧文是被利奥打伤的,利奥的行为已经损害了欧文的身体健康。虽然利奥打欧文一拳是为了救欧文,他的主观愿望是好的,但是他的行为造成的后果是严重的。法律不能因为一个人的愿望或者目的是好的,便免除他的一切责任。

艾莉:我不同意您的观点,我认为利奥不应该承担法律责任。

正如您所说,利奥打欧文不是故意想要伤害他,而是为了救欧文的命,是为了他好。如果利奥不打欧文一拳,不让欧文安静下来,根据溺水救人的常识,利奥很难把他救出来,说不定欧文就不是现在的受伤住院,而是直接没命了。

如果让利奥对此承担法律责任，对他不太公平，而且也会打击利奥以后帮助他人的热情和积极性。

爸爸：我们具体来讨论一下。如果当时利奥不入水营救，情况会怎么样？

艾莉：很难说，欧文可能凶多吉少。

爸爸：有这么严重吗？

艾莉：是的。欧文的游泳技术我很了解，非常一般，而且泳池的水又很深，脚抓不到地。

爸爸：当时他已经溺水了？

艾莉：欧文在水中游了很长时间，腿抽筋了，而且他学习游泳的时间不长，自救的知识和经验也不多，从当时的情况来看，他已经溺水了，很难自救，需要帮忙。

爸爸：我刚才好像听你说，当天游泳馆里的人不多。

艾莉：是的。因为当天不是休息日，时间也比较早，所以游泳馆里的人很少，而且当时大家都专注于游泳，根本没有发现欧文脚抽筋！

爸爸：也就是说，如果利奥不及时出手营救，欧文可能会溺水身亡或者遭受其他严重后果？

艾莉：完全有可能。

爸爸：看来当时的情况确实很紧急。

艾莉：是的，非常紧急！

爸爸：我有个问题。

艾莉：什么问题？

爸爸：利奥是游泳馆的救生员吗？

艾莉：不是。他很喜欢游泳，是游泳馆的常客，和大家都很熟。他平时很愿意帮助别人，所以不少人以为他是游泳馆的工作人员。

爸爸：明白了。

艾莉：这有什么区别吗？

爸爸：有些区别。如果利奥是游泳馆的救生员，营救欧文并保证欧文的安全就是他的本职工作。

艾莉：我明白了。利奥不是游泳馆的工作人员，所以他的行为属于帮助他人的行为，是在做好事。我当时也是想都没想就游过去了！

爸爸：所以也要给你点个赞！

艾莉：那倒不必。在那种情况下，大家都会这么做的，否则以后您也不放心让我一个人去游泳了。

爸爸：可是在营救欧文的过程中，利奥为什么要打欧文一拳呢？

艾莉：刚开始利奥没有打他，只是搂住了他的脖子。后来，因为欧文不停地挣扎，导致无法施救，利奥为了让他安静下来，以便顺利施救，才打了欧文一拳。

爸爸：如果当时欧文无法安静下来，结果会怎么样呢？

艾莉：我自己经常游泳，这个我最清楚。

爸爸：说说看。

艾莉：人溺水后身体会变得很重，同时深水里又没有着力点，再加上落水者身体又比较滑，所以施救本身非常困难。

爸爸：也就是说，如果落水的人挣扎，就会大大增加施救的难度？

艾莉：当然。这会让施救者付出更大的力气，容易导致施救者精疲力竭，最后无法成功施救。不仅如此，如果施救者不小心被溺水者抱住了，施救者不但无法进行营救，而且自己也可能被拖下水，导致施救者死亡。

爸爸：有这么严重？

艾莉：是的！人溺水后会变得非常紧张，此时他抓住任何东西都会像抓住救命稻草一样，死死不放，拼命往下拉，所以深水救人时常常会发生溺水者和施救者双亡的悲剧。

爸爸：所以营救溺水者时最好从后面抱住他，以免被溺水者拖下水？

艾莉：对！

爸爸：看来在当时的情况下，让欧文安静下来、不再挣扎是很有必要的了。

艾莉：不是很有必要，是必须！

爸爸：除了打晕欧文，没有其他更好的办法吗？

艾莉：我们的游泳教练说过，深水救人经常用这种方法。

爸爸：为什么？

艾莉：因为溺水的人由于高度紧张或者已经神志不清，

劝说或者其他办法都很难让他迅速安静下来。击打头部，让他在短时间内晕厥，安静下来，就能更顺利地实施营救，这也是"以小博大"吧。

爸爸：看来利奥也是迫不得已。

艾莉：在那种紧急的情况下，基本上没有其他方法。

爸爸：不过利奥的一拳导致欧文脑震荡，让他伤得也不轻。

艾莉：但是欧文的命保住了呀！受伤和失去生命相比哪个损失更大，这是显而易见的！

爸爸：利奥的一拳虽然打伤了欧文，给欧文造成了一定的损失，但是却保护了他的生命。换句话说，利奥的行为虽然造成了一定的损害，但是却保护了更大的利益。

艾莉：对的，而且还避免了利奥自己受"牵连"。

爸爸：利奥救人是做好事，应该鼓励，而且在这么紧急的情况下，利奥也没有其他更好的办法，所以，他打了欧文一拳也是情有可原。

艾莉：这么说，您同意我的意见了？

爸爸：等等！

艾莉：还有什么问题？

爸爸：虽然当时的情况很紧急，虽然利奥是在做好事，虽然利奥的一拳是迫不得已，虽然利奥的一拳避免了更大的损失，但是，你觉得他的行为有没有过当？

艾莉：什么是行为过当？

爸爸：行为过当是指采取的措施超过了必要的限度，导致了不必要的损失。或者说，为了达到需要的效果，没有必要采取后果这么严重的方法或者措施。

艾莉：行为过当会是什么后果？

爸爸：如果行为过当，超过了必要的限度，导致了更大的损失，即使行为人的主观愿望是为了帮助他人，行为人也要承担一定的法律责任。

艾莉：您能举个行为过当的例子吗？

爸爸：比如，司机驾驶大巴车行驶在高速路上，看见前面跑过一只小松鼠，司机紧急刹车，导致多位乘客受重伤。

艾莉：我同意，这是行为过当！即使做好事也不能不计后果，否则也会"好心办坏事"。

爸爸：对。

艾莉：这个以前您给我讲过，我都还记得。

爸爸：不错！那么利奥这一拳是不是可以轻点呢？如果"下手"不这么重，可能……

艾莉：在那么紧急的情况下，其实任何人，即便是像我这样经常游泳的人也会很紧张，很难控制自己的"轻重"，毕竟我们都不是专业的施救人员，也不是医生。

爸爸：嗯……

艾莉：想想看，如果当时利奥"犹犹豫豫"，顾虑这又顾虑那，既要选择部位又要仔细考虑轻重，可能就会错过救援的黄金时机，后果不堪设想！

爸爸：哈哈，有道理，毕竟是紧急救人，不是采花！

艾莉：其实利奥当时的行为可能都是下意识的，根本没那么多时间去考虑，换了我，估计也是一样。

爸爸：看来是我要求太高。

艾莉：对，我们不能做"事后诸葛亮"。

爸爸：假如让利奥承担一部分医疗费，你觉得怎么样？

艾莉：看来您还是"不死心"！

爸爸：我是说假如……

艾莉：正如前面我们讨论的，利奥的行为是做好事，而且下水救人本身就是一件非常危险的事情，如果再让他对此承担法律责任，那么以后遇到类似的事情大家可能都会"犹豫"了，这不应该是我们的社会所提倡的。

爸爸：同意！为了使公共利益、本人或者他人的人身和其他权利免受正在发生的危险，不得已而采取的损害较小利益以保护较大合法权益的行为，法律上称为紧急避险。紧急避险行为造成损害的，行为人不需要对此承担法律责任，但是紧急避险行为不能超过必要的限度，否则行为人需要承担一定的法律责任。

艾莉：欧耶！

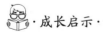
· 成长启示 ·

紧急避险的行为虽然造成了一定的损害，但是却保护了更大的利益，而且很多紧急避险的行为帮助他人消除了危险，是做好事，应该予以鼓励，因此行为人不应该对损害结果承担法律责任。但是，紧急避险不能超过必要的限度，如果超过必要限度，造成了不必要的损失，则行为人应该承担一定的法律责任。

·成长思考·

1. 利奥为什么打了欧文一拳？
2. 水中救人为什么很危险？
3. 遇到他人落水你会怎么办？

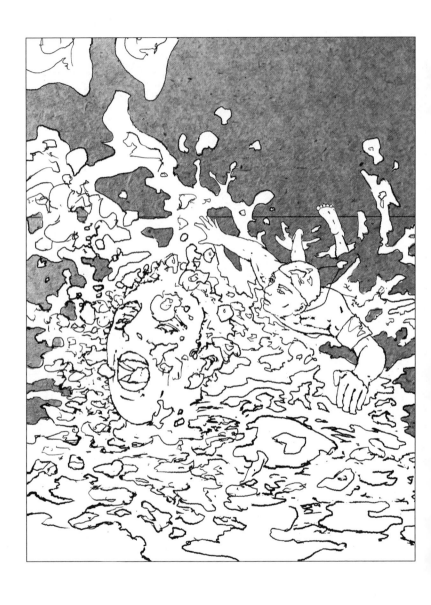

Chapter 6

Necessity

🦉 Reading Guide

When Ellie went to the gym for a swim the other day, an accident happened: Owen the bulky guy was drowning! Leo, eager to help, jumped into the pool immediately. Owen struggled desperately for air, kicking in every direction. Desperate to save him, Leo struck Owen and knocked him out. Was Owen successfully rescued? Why was Leo sullen and worried after saving Owen? When saving people from drowning, if the rescuer had to take some urgent measures but accidentally harmed the drowning person, should the rescuer bear legal responsibility?

Ellie had always loved swimming — and she was good at it! When she was in fifth grade, she swam for her school's swim team, and while she didn't continue on the swim team when she transferred to a new school, Ellie would still go to the swimming pool near her house to practice.

One day after school, as usual, Ellie went to the pool for a swim. It was a quiet day at the pool, perhaps because it was not the weekends; most of her best friends were not there. However, Ellie did see Leo who was a frequent visitor to this pool. He once told Ellie that he had been swimming at this pool for nearly twenty years.

Not only was Leo a fantastic swimmer, but he also loved to teach. When he was not busy, Leo would often help others with their swimming skills. He also reminded people that swimming in the water for a long time could easily cause muscles to stiffen and cause foot or leg cramps. He told everyone, "If you have foot or leg cramps, don't worry. Keep calm, take a deep breath, dive into the water, float on the surface of the water, grab your toes with your hands, and stretch them in the direction of your body. Repeat this motion several times, and then try to take a break by the poolside as soon as possible." Leo seemed like the perfect fit for a swimming coach!

"Hey, Ellie, I saved Lane Three just for you today!" Leo yelled across the pool — he was always so enthusiastic!

Three was Ellie's favorite number, lane three was also Ellie and Leo's favorite lane.

"Thank you for thinking of me! I hope you can still reserve Lane Three for me on the weekend. It gets really busy around here!"

"But you won't be lonely. Owen is in Lane Four today," Leo winked and added.

That was when Ellie felt the currents coming from Lane Four; Owen was swimming strenuously next to her.

Owen was very tall, about 6 feet 2 inches (about 188 cm), and weighed nearly 210 pounds (about 95kg). He was kind of a "bulky guy." He had just learned how to swim and was very enthusiastic. The coach said that Owen was a fast learner, but due to the fact that he wasn't used to a lot of exercise, his muscles were tight and tense when swimming. However, Owen had improved a lot.

After warming up, Ellie jumped into the pool and swam proficiently. The water temperature was a bit low today, but it was the temperature that Ellie liked. Touch the wall, turn around, touch the wall again ... After a few laps, Ellie felt a bit more warmed up, and it seemed that her body was almost completely stretched out. From the corner of her eyes, Ellie saw that Owen was about half the pool away from her.

"It feels like a good day to practice today. I think I'll practice for a little longer," Ellie thought to herself.

At the end of a lap, Ellie just touched the wall and was ready to turn around when she suddenly heard a cry. Ellie stopped, held onto the side of the pool with one hand, and turned to see what happened. She saw a huge splash in the center of the pool. Owen was desperately hitting the surface of the water, causing large splashes, and murmuring sounds came out of his mouth, "Help me! Help me!"

"It's Owen, he's drowning!" Years of swimming experience allowed Ellie to make an instant judgment.

Ellie organized her thoughts and was about to help with the rescue when she saw a familiar figure fly into the pool. It was Leo! He quickly swam up behind Owen and suddenly caught Owen's neck from behind. All of a sudden, Owen stopped screaming, and the pool returned to the peaceful mode it had been in. The two were slowly moving to the side of the pool when all of a sudden, the splashing started again! It seemed that Owen and Leo were mingling together. However, Owen quickly became calm again and seemed asleep. At this point, Ellie arrived next to them quickly and helped Leo drag Owen onto the poolside. Ellie had heard from others before that people would become very heavy after drowning, but she didn't expect Owen to be this heavy! A few people on the poolside immediately came around, and after a few busy minutes, Owen was finally dragged onto the side of the pool. Owen's face was deadly pale, and he was unconscious. Leo quickly did the cardiopulmonary resuscitation on him, and Owen regained consciousness. After sending Owen to the hospital in the ambulance, everyone let out a heavy breath and surrounded Leo, asking him about what exactly happened.

Leo said, "I hugged Owen from behind, and it started off just fine, but Owen's arms were very long, and he suddenly grabbed my arms with his backhand and pulled me down, making me unable to help him. So, I struck him in the head. Owen fainted, and I dragged him to the side of the pool. Now that I think about it, it is such a scary situation! Even after swimming for so many years, this is the first time I have encountered such a situation!" Leo fell silent.

After a few days, Ellie went to the swimming pool again, but she did not see Leo. The swimming pool administrator told Ellie that Leo had been in a bad mood for the past few days. He was upset with himself because he felt bad about hitting Owen when he was saving him. Although his life was no longer in danger, Owen had a concussion and needed to stay in hospital for several days — that was going to be very expensive.

Ellie was concerned about the situation. When she got home, she started chatting with her father about it.

Ellie: Dad, do you think Leo should be held legally responsible for happened?

Dad: I think he should. Leo harmed Owen. Leo's behavior already violated Owen's physical health. Although Leo stunned Owen in order to save him and his subjective intentions were good, his actions caused serious consequences. The law cannot exempt one from all of his duties simply because one's intentions or purposes were meant to be good.

Ellie: I disagree with you. I don't think Leo should be held legally responsible.

As you said, Leo stunned Owen not to hurt him intentionally, but to save Owen's life. If Leo had not punched Owen, there would have been no way to calm Owen, and anyone who has the common sense of saving people knows that Leo would either have a hard time rescuing Owen or wouldn't have been able to at all. By then, maybe Owen would not simply have been injured or hospitalized but would have been dead! If Leo is held legally responsible, it will be too unfair to him, and it will also discourage Leo's enthusiasm in helping others in the future.

Dad: Let's talk about it more specifically. What would have happened if Leo hadn't jumped into the water to help?

Ellie: It's hard to say what would have happened, but Owen probably would have been in more trouble.

Dad: Was it that serious?

Ellie: Yes. I know how Owen swims. He is not the most

skilled swimmer. Plus, the pool is deep, and one's feet can't touch the bottom.

Dad: At that time, was he drowning already?

Ellie: Owen had been swimming in the water for a long time, so his legs were cramping. Also, he hadn't learned how to swim for long, so he was not yet knowledgeable and experienced enough to rescue himself. From the situation at the time, he was already drowning, and it was difficult for him to save himself without any help.

Dad: I remember hearing you say that there were not many people at the swimming pool that day.

Ellie: Yes. Because it was a weekday, there were very few people at the swimming pool. Plus, everyone was focused on swimming at the time, and no one realized that Owen was drowning!

Dad: So, can I interpret this as "had Leo not rescued him in time, Owen may have been drowned or suffered other serious consequences"?

Ellie: It was entirely possible.

Dad: It seems that the situation at the time was really urgent.

Ellie: Yes, it really was very urgent!

Dad: I have a question.

Ellie: What's the question?

Dad: Was Leo a lifeguard at the swimming pool?

Ellie: No. He loves swimming and is a frequent visitor to the swimming pool; he was also close friends with everyone there. Leo is always eager to help others — so much that many people thought he was a staff member at the pool.

Dad: I see.

Ellie: Does that make any difference?

Dad: It does make a difference. If Leo had been a lifeguard at the swimming pool, it would have been his job to rescue and ensure the safety of Owen.

Ellie: I see. Leo was not a staff member at the swimming pool, so his behavior should be considered as helping others. He rescued Owen out of his good nature. In that situation, I also reacted quickly and swam right over to help!

Dad: So, a big thumbs up to you!

Ellie: I was not fishing for compliments. In that situation, everyone would have tried to help; otherwise, you would not feel safe for letting me go swimming alone.

Dad: But in the process of saving Owen, why did Leo hit Owen?

Ellie: Leo didn't hit him at first, he just grabbed Owen's neck. Later, because Owen was twisting violently and made it difficult to rescue him, Leo punched Owen in order to calm him down for a smooth rescue.

Dad: If Owen had not been able to calm down at the time, what would have happened?

Ellie: I swim a lot, so I know all about what would have happened.

Dad: Tell me about it.

Ellie: When drowning, the human body becomes very heavy, and it is difficult to maintain a grip on the person, so it is very difficult to rescue him in the first place.

Dad: In other words, if a drowning person struggles, it will greatly increase the difficulty of rescue?

Ellie: Of course. This means that the rescuer will experience greater difficulty trying to rescue the drowning person, and it could easily lead to the exhaustion of the rescuer and eventually the failure of the rescue. Further, if the rescuer is accidentally dragged by the drowning person, both the victim and the rescuer may drown.

Dad: Is it really that serious?

Ellie: Yes! Once a person is drowning, he or she will become very nervous. At this time, he or she will try to grasp onto anything for support and pull whatever he or she is holding into. So, among rescues in deep water, there have been many tragedies where both the rescuer and the rescued died.

Dad: So, when you are rescuing a drowning person, is it best to hug the person from behind to avoid being dragged underwater?

Ellie: Yes!

Dad: It seems that under the circumstances, it was necessary to find a way to calm Owen down and make him stop struggling desperately.

Ellie: It was not just "seemingly necessary." It was very necessary!

Dad: Was there any better way to do so apart from stunning Owen?

Ellie: Our swimming coach once said that this method was often used in deep water rescues.

Dad: Why?

Ellie: A drowning person is understandably panicked and not thinking straight, so stunning him or her for a short period of time so that the rescuer can carry out the rescue more smoothly is important. This is also "throwing a sprat to catch a mackerel."

Dad: Looks like Owen was out of other choices.

Ellie: In an urgent situation like this one, there is basically no other solution.

Dad: But Leo's punch caused Owen's to be concussed.

Owen was badly hurt.

Ellie: But at least Owen is alive! When comparing being injured to the loss of life, it is obvious which one is the greater loss!

Dad: Even though Leo's punch injured Owen and caused loss to Owen, the action actually protected his life. In other words, Leo's actions did cause loss for Owen, but it actually protected a greater interest.

Ellie: Right, and it also avoided putting Leo's life in danger.

Dad: Leo's action of saving people's lives was a good thing, and it should be encouraged. In such an urgent situation, Leo also had no other choice, so it was justifiable that he stunned Owen.

Ellie: So, do you agree with my argument?

Dad: Hold on!

Ellie: What's the problem?

Dad: Although the situation was very urgent at the time and although Leo's punch was a necessary move to prevent death and eventually protected Owen from greater loss, do you think his behavior and actions were excessive?

Ellie: What is considered as an excessive behavior?

Dad: An excessive behavior means that the measures taken exceed the necessary limits and cause unnecessary loss. In other words, in order to achieve the desired effect, it is not necessary to take such a serious method or measure.

Ellie: What are the consequences of excessive behaviors?

Dad: If an excessive behavior exceeds the necessary limits and results in greater loss, then even if the subjective intention is to help others, the perpetrator must still bear certain legal responsibilities.

Ellie: Can you give an example of an excessive behavior?

Dad: For example, a bus driver drove on the highway and braked urgently to avoid an animal running in front of the bus — that action unintentionally cased many passengers to be seriously injured.

Ellie: I agree that this is an example of an excessive behavior! Even if you have a good intention, you can't just ignore the consequences; otherwise, you will be doing bad things out of good intentions.

Dad: Right.

Ellie: You have told me this before, and I still remember it.

Dad: Good job! So, could Leo's punch have been lighter? If the punch hadn't been so powerful, maybe …

Ellie: In such an urgent a situation, in fact, anyone, even people who often swim like me, would be very nervous. It would be difficult to control the "lightness" of the punch. After all, we are not professional rescuers, and nor are we doctors.

Dad: Hmm …

Ellie: Think about it. If Leo had been hesitant at the time, carefully choosing the body part to grab onto and meticulously calculating everything, then Leo might have missed his best opportunity to rescue. The consequences would have been unimaginable!

Dad: Ha-ha, that sounds reasonable. After all, it was an emergency rescue, not a flower picking event!

Ellie: In fact, Leo's actions at the time might all have been subconscious. There was really not much time to think carefully. If it were me, I would probably have done the same thing.

Dad: It seems that my standards for the rescue was too high.

Ellie: Yes, we can't judge every detail after an emergency has happened.

Dad: What if we let Leo be held responsible for part of the medical bills?

Ellie: It seems that you still haven't given up on your side!

Dad: Just hypothetically …

Ellie: Like we have discussed earlier, Leo was trying to help others. Plus, it's a very dangerous thing to save people underwater in the first place. If he has to bear so much responsibility, then when people encounter similar situation in the future, they might become hesitant about taking actions to rescue others. This should not be advocated by our society.

Dad: I totally agree! If a person is compelled to commit an act in an emergency to avert an immediate danger to the interests of the public or his own or another person's rights, thus causing damage, this act of damaging minor interests to protect the greater interests as a last resort is called an act of necessity. The perpetrator does not need to bear legal responsibility for damage caused by an act of necessity, but the act cannot exceed the necessary limits; otherwise, the perpetrator still needs to bear certain legal responsibilities.

Ellie: Yay!

 Growth Revelation

Although acts of necessity might result in some loss or harm, they protect the greater interests of others and in many situations, save others from dangers. Because they are meant to be beneficial, these acts should be encouraged, and therefore, the perpetrator does not need to bear legal responsibility for such damage. However, acts of necessity cannot exceed the necessary limits. If they exceed the necessary limits and cause unnecessary loss, the perpetrator will also have to bear certain legal liabilities.

❓ Think and Consider

1. Why did Leo punch Owen?

2. Why is it dangerous to save people in the water?

3. What would you do if you encounter a similar situation of someone drowning?

第七章
收回录取通知书

·导读·

L高中夏令营归来,艾莉萌发了申请L高中的想法,没想到,这个想法居然得到了妈妈的支持!艾莉带着美好的憧憬进入了梦乡,梦中艾莉收到了心仪已久的L高中的录取通知书,从此她的生活发生了改变……艾莉的梦想能成真吗?学校可以收回已经发出的录取通知书吗?

L学校是一所知名的私立学校,它的夏令营远近闻名,参加L学校的夏令营一直是艾莉的梦想。妈妈答应她,只要她这学期表现好,就资助她参加夏令营。当艾莉拿到L学校夏令营的录取通知书,尤其是得知自己打败了众多竞争对手的时候,她高兴得一夜都没怎么合眼,早早地就把行李准备好了。

一个月的夏令营生活如做梦一样飞快地结束了。回到家里,艾莉迫不及待地给妈妈讲自己在夏令营的生活,讲百年老校的红砖绿草,讲像《哈利·波特》中的霍格沃茨魔法学校一样的图书馆,讲学校商店琳琅满目的纪念品。最重要的是,L学校的老师非常鼓励同学们去探索,只要你有任何好的点子，老师都会给你详细的指导和帮助，让你始终充满探索的激情。

"我要是能在这样的学校读书就好了！"艾莉喃喃自语道。

看着女儿陶醉的样子，艾莉妈妈看出了她的几分心思。

吃晚饭时，妈妈说："艾莉，你现在的学校很好，而且你在这个学校又有很多朋友，你真的想去L学校吗？据说申请L学校很难啊！"

沉默了一会，艾莉说："我现在的学校确实很好，我在学校里也有很多朋友，但是我还是很想去L学校读书。我知道申请成功很难，但是我想试一试。您不是常说，试了不一定成功，但不试一定没有好结果嘛！"

妈妈想了想，说："好的，我同意，但是，"妈妈故意顿了顿，继续说道："前提是你要自己准备申请资料。今天太晚了，吃完饭赶紧上床睡觉吧。"

听了妈妈的话，艾莉高兴得直点头："好，我一定努力，加油，耶！"

一个月的夏令营生活虽然有趣，但艾莉也确实太累了，头一碰枕头，她就进入了梦乡。

迷迷糊糊中，一道白光闪过，好像是一个星期天的早上，初雪过后，天气晴朗，空气格外清新。门铃响了，艾莉打开房门，一股寒气扑面而来，熟悉的邮递员递过来一封信。一看到信封上的"L学校"几个字，艾莉不顾屋外的寒冷，赶紧打开信件。艾莉一口气读了好几遍信，她简直不敢相信自己的眼睛，这是真的吗?!

"妈妈，妈妈，快来，我被录取了，我被 L 学校录取了!"可能是天气太冷，也可能是太激动，艾莉的声音颤抖着。

艾莉的妈妈爸爸冲下了楼，抢过信大声读了起来，一家人紧紧地抱在一起。一想到自己这段时间为了申请高中，准备考试、撰写申请材料、参加面试，可以说是起早贪黑，全家甚至为此放弃了外出休假，艾莉禁不住流下了热泪，爸爸妈妈也高兴得不停地恭喜艾莉。

接下来的几天里，艾莉的生活可以说是眼花缭乱。朋友们纷纷打电话、发邮件表示祝贺，亲戚们上门道喜，哥哥姐姐送上特别的礼物，爷爷奶奶专程飞过来，还给她买了一台新电脑。艾莉更是脸上挂着微笑，口里哼着小曲儿，走路时脚下好像装了弹簧似的，整个人都沉浸在无比的放松和幸福之中。

一天午后，艾莉正在收拾行李，妈妈下班回到家。

"妈妈，这几天是 L 学校最后的回复时间，我们是否要回复学校?"艾莉问道。

"好的，既然你选择了 L 学校，今天就回复他们吧，同时也回绝其他几个学校，免得影响别人。"妈妈回答道。

"好嘞，我这就去回复。"说着，艾莉上楼回复邮件去了。

第二天早上，一家人刚刚起床，门铃响了，快递员送来了 L 学校的快递。

"还有什么资料需要邮寄给我？难道是入学指南？"艾莉满腹疑惑，倚着门读了起来。

读着读着，空气好像突然凝固了。"亲爱的艾莉同学，我是 L 学校的招生办公室主任。我很抱歉地通知您，由于我校计算机系统出现了紊乱，错误地给您发了录取通知书。这个通知书应该是发给另外一个艾莉同学的，所以很抱歉……"

"妈妈！"艾莉大叫了一声，一下子惊醒了，原来是一场梦。

打开灯，看看表，已经是凌晨一点多了，周围一片寂静，满天星斗，艾莉一身冷汗。这一夜，她再也没能入睡，眼前总是浮现出 L 学校的录取通知书和招生办主任的信。

早饭时，艾莉把昨晚的噩梦告诉了爸爸。爸爸调侃道："看来美梦即使在梦里也难以成真啊！"

看到艾莉沮丧地嘟着嘴，爸爸赶紧安慰道："别着急，梦经常是反的，你的梦想一定能成真！"

爸爸的安慰还是不能让艾莉释怀，父女俩不由自主地讨论起来。

艾莉：爸爸，您觉得学校有权利收回录取通知书吗？
爸爸：你觉得呢？

艾莉：我觉得学校没有这个权利。

爸爸：说说你的理由。

艾莉：录取通知书是学校发出的，而且我也收到了，学校和我之间已经形成了一定的契约关系。

学校说是计算机系统的问题导致录取通知书发错了，即使这是事实，这也是由于学校自己的过错造成的，学校应该对自己的错误行为承担责任，不能让学生对学校的工作失误背"黑锅"。

录取通知书里，学校已经明确表示同意录取我，我也因此拒绝了其他学校。如果L学校就这样把录取通知书收回了，会导致我错过到其他理想学校学习的机会，这对我今后的学习生活可能产生不利的影响，对我不公平，社会不能纵容这种伤害他人的行为。

爸爸：就这些理由？

艾莉：暂时就这些。

爸爸：我倒是认为学校有权收回录取通知书。

录取通知书是学校单方面发给你的，既然是学校单方面发出的，那么学校也有权单方面收回。

学校只是向你发出了录取通知书，还没有向你收取任何费用，因此，学校不应该受到约束。

录取通知书虽然发给你了，但是你还没到学校报到，你还不是学校的学生。即使你报到了，成了学校的学生，学校也有权开除学生，更何况你还不是学校的学生。

艾莉：我认为您的理由不成立。

录取通知书虽然是学校单方面发出的，但它明确是向我发出的，因此，它已经不仅仅是学校一方的事情，已经涉及学校和我两方的权利和义务。

录取通知书明确表示学校同意录取我前去上学，这是学校给我的权利，学校也就有了相应的义务。因此，我有权利来上学，学校也有义务接收我上学。

您说，学校还没有收取学费，所以学校不应该受到约束。我觉得，即使一个行为没有给自己带来任何好处，但是它可能给别人带来很大的损失，那么这个行为同样也应该受到约束。比如，您把别人的车砸坏了，您可能没有因此得到什么好处，但是您的行为导致了别人的财产损失，您的这个行为同样应该被禁止。

您说，即使我报到了，成了学校的学生，学校也有权开除学生，更何况我还不是学校的学生。但是我认为，学校虽然有权开除学生，但也不能随随便便地开除学生，只有在学生实施了违法或者严重违反学校纪律的行为时，学校才可以开除学生。我没有做错任何事儿，学校当然不可以开除我或者收回我的录取通知书。

爸爸：你反驳得很有力度，看来是因为有切肤之痛啊！

艾莉：老爸，不要在我伤口上撒盐，好吧。

爸爸：好的，不过砸车子的例子有点极端。

艾莉：我想表达的意思是：是否承担责任不应该以自己

是否获得利益为前提。

爸爸：很好，那么我们来具体探讨一下。你有什么问题吗？

艾莉：有的。录取通知书是什么呢？

爸爸：录取通知书是学校发出的，表示其同意接受某个学生来学校读书的一份法律文件。

艾莉：那么，这是不是意味着录取通知书是学校给学生的一份承诺，承诺其同意接受学生入学？

爸爸：应该是这样。

艾莉：既然是承诺就应该遵守！

爸爸：如果承诺不被遵守会怎么样呢？

艾莉：您的钱可能就不敢存银行了。

爸爸：为什么？

艾莉：因为您怕银行没有信用，不遵守承诺，到时您取不出钱。

爸爸：那倒是挺吓人！还有什么呢？

艾莉：剪草工不敢给我们家剪草了，因为怕我们不给他开支票。

爸爸：那我们去餐厅吃饭可能也有问题了。厨师不肯先给我们做饭，担心我们吃完饭不付钱。

艾莉：可我们先付钱又会担心厨师溜掉，这不是成了死循环了吗？

爸爸：可见，诚信对一个人很重要，对一个公司很重要，对一个社会更重要。

艾莉：是的，一个人如果没有了信用，就不会有朋友了。

爸爸：一个公司如果没有了信用，就会失去客户；如果整个社会都没有信用了，我们的衣食住行都会出问题，生活会一团糟。

艾莉：看来承诺必须要遵守！

爸爸：扯得似乎有点远，回到我们要讨论的具体问题上。如果学校收回录取通知书，你会遭受什么损失吗？

艾莉：在梦中，我去学校的机票都买了，庆祝的聚会也举行了，朋友们的礼物我也收了。

爸爸：最重要的是，你因此已经拒绝了其他学校的录取通知书。

艾莉：是的，所有这些都是因为我相信了这份 L 学校的录取通知书，所以它不能被收回。

爸爸：看来 L 学校是要慎重决定！那么，你认为录取通知书应该包括哪些内容呢？

艾莉：我想，它首先应该明确表示同意录取我前去上学吧。

爸爸：对的，这是必须的。如果通知书说"正在考虑或者你需要等待"，那它还不能算是录取通知书。还有其他的吗？

艾莉：梦里通知书的其他内容我记不清了。

爸爸：你凭着录取通知书就可以准备入学了，想想看，你还需要知道些什么呢？

艾莉：它应该告诉我入学时间。另外，我还需要知道它录取我上几年级，降级我肯定不干，哈哈。

爸爸：要列明学费是多少吗？

艾莉：这个必须要有，太贵了我出不起。

爸爸：这些基本内容都应该包括在录取通知书中。如果一个录取通知书不包括这些内容，你还无法明确是否已被录取或者你还不知道具体该怎么操作，那么它还不是一个有约束力的录取通知书。

艾莉：懂了。我有个问题。

爸爸：什么问题？

艾莉：如果学生拿到了录取通知书，但他一直不来报到，那学校该怎么办呢？难道学校要一直等他吗？

爸爸：一直等对学校不公平吧？

艾莉：是的，可能还会影响学校的下一步工作安排。

爸爸：所以通常情况下，录取通知书都会明确要求你在什么时间回复或者在什么时间之前报到。

艾莉：这就是所谓的最后期限？

爸爸：是的。

艾莉：如果过期不回复或者不来报到会怎么样呢？

爸爸：那学校自然不再受这份录取通知书的约束，它可以补录其他的同学或者把这份录取通知书作废。

艾莉：明白了！现实中真的会出现类似我梦中的计算机出错的情况吗？

爸爸：可能会有出错的情况，只是出错的原因各种各样。

艾莉：那该怎么办？

爸爸：一方面，学校会加强管理，尽量减少或避免出错；另一方面，学校也可能会采取一些措施，增强自我保护。比如，有些学校会在通知书中提示，在收到学生明确回复后录取通知书才生效。还有的学校规定，在收到学生的保证金或学费后通知书才生效，等等。

艾莉：看来以后我要仔细阅读录取通知书，尤其要仔细阅读重要的提示。

爸爸：希望你梦想成真！

艾莉：不过这样的梦我还是不要再做了！

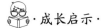
·成长启示·

诚信是一个社会的基础，诚信对一个人、一个公司，乃至整个社会都很重要。

学校录取通知书是学校同意接受学生入学的重要法律文件，是学校对学生的承诺，不应轻易地违反。录取通知书通常包括同意学生入学、入学时间、年级、学费等主要内容，有些录取通知书还包括一些重要提示，学生要严格按照录取通知书的要求操作，否则可能会给自己带来麻烦。

· 成长思考·

1. 艾莉做了一个什么样的梦?
2. 你是如何理解学校录取通知书的?
3. 你觉得学校录取通知书应该包括哪些内容?

Chapter 7

Taking Back the Offer

📖 Reading Guide

Returning from a summer camp at L High School, Ellie asked her parents if she could apply to L High School and, to her surprise, her mother agreed! That night, Ellie went to sleep full of excitement about what the future might hold; she dreamt about receiving the long-awaited admission letter from L High School and how her life might change. Would Ellie's dream come true? Can a school withdraw an offer letter that has already been issued?

L High School was a famous private school with a particularly well-known summer program. Ellie had wanted to attend L High School's summer camp for a long time, and her mom had promised Ellie that if Ellie was on her best behavior throughout the spring semester, she would allow Ellie to attend the camp. The day that Ellie received her acceptance letter for the summer camp was one of the happiest days of her life — her hands even shook as she read the letter! She couldn't sleep that night, and she began planning what she would take the following morning.

The month that Ellie spent at the summer camp flew by. When she got home, Ellie couldn't stop telling her mom about her life at the summer camp, describing the beautiful campus with a library that looked like Hogwarts while also recounting all the cute souvenirs in the school bookstore. Moreover, Ellie was really impressed with the way the teachers there encouraged students to explore topics they were interested in. Teachers would then discuss what the students had learned, ensuring that the students stay curious and keep exploring.

"Wouldn't it be amazing if I could actually go to school there?" Ellie mumbled.

Seeing Ellie's dreamy expression, her mom knew that Ellie was serious.

Later, while eating dinner, Mom asked, "Ellie, you are currently at an amazing school, and you have so many friends here. Do you really want to go to L High School? I mean, it is surely really competitive and hard to get into."

After a short silence, Ellie said, "It is true that I am currently at a wonderful school where I have lots of friends, but I still want to go to L School for high school. I know it is hard to get into, but I want to give it a try. You've always taught me that trying might not lead to success, but there would be no success without trying."

Mom stopped for a minute and nodded. "OK, I agree, but ..." she hesitated on purpose, "you have to prepare your resume and application materials on your own. It's getting late today. Get some sleep after your meal."

Ellie couldn't stop grinning and nodding, "Of course! I will work very hard! Yay!"

While her month of summer camp had been lots of fun, it had also been a lot of work, and Ellie was very tired. When her head touched the pillow, she instantly fell into a deep sleep with vivid dreams ...

Accompanied by a blur of white light, Ellie seemed to wake up on a Sunday morning. After the first snow day of the year, the weather was nice, and the air was crisp and fresh. The doorbell rang. Ellie opened the door to greet the postman as he handed over a letter. When she saw the L High School logo on the package, Ellie disregarded the freezing weather outside and quickly opened the letter. She read it several times in one breath but still could not believe her eyes. Could this be true?

"Mom, Mom, come! I got the offer. I got into L High School!" Maybe it was because the weather was too cold, or maybe it was due to excitement, but Ellie's voice was quivering.

Mom and Dad rushed downstairs, grabbed the letter from her hand, and read it out aloud. The family held tight together. Throughout the application process, Ellie had shed tears as she worked to assemble the required materials. Preparing for the exams, writing application essays, and attending interviews all meant that Ellie had woken up early and went to bed late in order to get every piece of her materials in by the deadline. The family even gave up their vacation. Tears of joy rolled down Ellie's face as her parents congratulated her.

Over the next several days, Ellie's life could be described as dazzling. Friends congratulated her through phone calls and text messages. Relatives came to Ellie's house for a mini celebration, and Ellie's cousins all brought special gifts for her. Grandpa and Grandma came to visit and even bought her a new laptop as a gift! Ellie couldn't stop smiling as she skipped down the street; it was like springs were attached to the bottom of her shoes. She was incredibly relaxed and overwhelmed with joy.

One afternoon, when Ellie was packing up, Mom came home from work.

"Mom, the deadline to accept L High School's offer is coming up. Should we reply to them today?" Ellie asked.

"Yes. If we choose to go to L High School, we should reply

to them today and turn down other schools' offers so that other students on the waiting list can receive a formal notice as soon as possible," Mom answered.

"Good idea, I will go do that right now," Ellie said, going upstairs to reply the e-mail.

The next morning, when the family just got out of bed, the doorbell rang, and the postman handed the family another package from L High School.

"What other information did they need to mail to me? Is it a 'Back-to-School Survival Guide?'" Opening the envelope, Ellie read the letter while leaning against the door.

She read it slowly, and the air grew heavy, "Dear Ellie, I am the director of the admissions office of L High School. I am sorry to inform you that, due to a mistake in the computer system of our school, we sent you the wrong notice. This notice should have been sent to another Ellie, and I sincerely apologize …"

"Mom!" Ellie screamed, feeling as if her world was collapsing. She sat up suddenly, realizing that it was all but a dream.

Ellie quickly reached over to turn on the light. Looking at the alarm clock, Ellie saw it was just past 1:00 am. It had all been a lovely dream turned into a horrible nightmare. Now awake, she looked at the stars, unable to sleep for the rest of the night.

At breakfast, Ellie told her father about the nightmare. Dad teased, "It seems that a dream doesn't even come true in a dream!"

Looking at Ellie's disappointed face, her father quickly comforted her, "Don't worry, dreams and nightmares are often the opposite of reality. I know that you will work hard, and I think that you will achieve your goal of getting into L school!"

While she appreciated her father's attempt to comfort her, Ellie still had trouble letting go of the dream, so they decided to have a long discussion.

Ellie: Dad, do you think the school in my dream had the right to rescind an offer of admission?

Dad: What is your opinion?

Ellie: I don't think it had the right to do that.

Dad: What are your reasons?

Ellie: The acceptance letter was issued by the school, and I had just accepted their offer before I received the second letter rescinding it. In my opinion, the school and I had formed a certain contractual relationship.

The school said they sent the wrong admission's notice because of an error in their system. Even if this had been the truth, it happened because of the school. The school should have taken responsibility for its own mistakes and should not have let the students suffer due to the school's mistakes.

In the acceptance letter, the school clearly agreed to accept me, and I therefore turned down other schools' offers. If L High School withdrew the acceptance letter, I would miss the opportunity to attend other prestigious schools. This might have a negative impact on my future education and life. It would be unfair to me, and society cannot condone such wrong and hurtful behaviors.

Dad: Are these all your reasons?

Ellie: For the time being.

Dad: Well, I would think that the school had the right to take back the offer.

The admission letter was unilaterally sent to you by the school. Since it was unilaterally issued by the school, the school had the right to unilaterally withdraw it.

The school just sent you an offer letter and had not charged you any fee or tuition yet, so the school is not necessarily obligated to continue with their original acceptance.

Although the offer letter was sent to you, you had not yet been officially enrolled in the school. Even if you had been to the orientation or had become a student at the school, the school would still have the right to expel its students, not to mention that you were not a student of the school yet.

Ellie: I think your reasons are not valid.

Although the admission letter was issued unilaterally by the school, it was clearly sent to me. Therefore, it not only involved the school, but also involved the rights and obligations of both the school and me.

The admission offer clearly stated that the school agreed to enroll me to the school. I thus became entitled to get enrolled, and the school had corresponding obligations. Therefore, I had the right to go to school, and the school was also obliged to accept me.

You said that the school had not charged any tuition yet, so the school should not have been bound. But even if an action would not benefit the person who took the action, if it may cause great loss to others, then such behavior should still be constrained. For example, if you break someone else's car, you may not be benefited in any way, but your behavior leads to the loss of property of others. Such behavior should also be banned.

You also mentioned that even after one had been to the school and become a student of the school, the school would still have the right to expel the student, not to mention that I was not a student of the school yet. However, I believe that although the school has the right to expel its students, it should not be allowed to expel students whenever they want to. Only when a student has committed illegal actions or serious violations of school rules can the school expel him or her. I have not done anything wrong, and therefore, the school can't expel me or take back my offer letter.

Dad: Wow, your arguments are very strong! It seems that the dream has left you with a really painful impression!

Ellie: Hey Dad, please don't rub salt in my wound, OK?!

Dad: Alright, but the example of burglarizing a car was a little extreme.

Ellie: What I wanted to say was that "whether or not you should bear the responsibility is not based on whether you are benefiting."

Dad: Very good. Then let's talk about it more specifically. Do you have any questions to ask?

Ellie: Yes. The first question: what does an admission notice, or an offer, do?

Dad: An offer is a legal document issued by the school to a student which indicates that the school agrees to accept the student to receive a proper education there.

Ellie: Does this mean that the admission notice is a promise from the school to the student, a promise to accept the student into the school?

Dad: It should be so.

Ellie: Since it is a promise, it should be kept.

Dad: What happens when promises are not kept?

Ellie: Then, for example, I wouldn't dare to deposit my money in the bank.

Dad: Why not?

Ellie: Because I would be afraid that the bank is not in good financial standing and would not have the ability to return my money when I need it.

Dad: That would be quite scary. What else?

Ellie: The lawn mower would not want to mow the lawn for our family, because he would be afraid that we would not give him a check after his work.

Dad: Then we may encounter a problem when going to a restaurant. The chef would refuse to cook for us, worrying that we won't pay for the meal.

Ellie: On the other hand, if the customers pay first, they might worry that the cooks aren't going to make the meal for them. Isn't this an infinite loop?

Dad: It is obvious that honesty is important to a person, to a company, and most importantly, to a society.

Ellie: Yes, if a person isn't credible, then he or she would not have any friends.

Dad: If a company does not have credit, it will have no

customers. If the whole society doesn't have credit, then every part of our lives will become problematic and a giant mess.

Ellie: It seems that promises must be kept!

Dad: After so many hypothetical examples, we should bring it back to the specific topic that we were discussing. If the school retracted its offer letter, what losses would you endure?

Ellie: In my dream, I bought the plane ticket to the school, the celebration party was already held, and the gifts from my friends were also opened.

Dad: The most important thing was that you had rejected the admission notices of other schools.

Ellie: Yes, all of these things happened because I believed that this offer letter was my golden ticket to attending the L High School. Therefore, it should not be retracted.

Dad: Looks like L School need to think twice in such a situation! So, in your opinion, what should an admission notice include?

Ellie: I think it should first explicitly agree to accept me into the school.

Dad: Yes, this is a must. If a notice says, "We are considering having you as a member of our future class" or "you need to wait for further notice," then it is not an admission notice. What else?

Ellie: I can't remember exactly what was on the offer from my dream.

Dad: You can start preparing to attend the school upon receiving the admission letter. Thank about it — what else do you need to know?

Ellie: It should tell me the time that I need to report to the school. Moreover, I still need to know which grade or class I have been committed to. I will definitely not accept an offer that offers me a spot a year or two from now.

Dad: Should it mention anything about tuition?

Ellie: That must be mentioned. If it is too expensive, then I can't afford it.

Dad: These basic contents should be included in the offer letter. If an offer does not include this information, one cannot be sure of whether or not he or she is accepted or may not know how exactly to complete all the procedures. Then, it is not a trustworthy admission notice.

Ellie: I understand, but I have one more question.

Dad: What is the question?

Ellie: What if a student gets the offer letter but does not respond to it promptly? Should the school continue to wait?

Dad: Wouldn't it be unfair to make the school wait?

Ellie: Yes, and it may affect the school's working schedule.

Dad: So, generally, there will be a clear rule in the

acceptance letter telling you when to reply to the letter or when to report to the school.

Ellie: Is it the so-called "deadline"?

Dad: Yes.

Ellie: What will happen if I don't reply by the deadline or don't report to school orientations?

Dad: Then, the school should not be and is not restricted by its offer anymore. It has the right to send a new offer to another student on the wait list or nullify the current offer.

Ellie: Got it! In reality, is it possible for what happened in my dream to happen, where the school experienced a technical difficulty and sent the offer mistakenly?

Dad: That is possible, but there are many different ways and reasons for mistakes to happen.

Ellie: Then what should the school do?

Dad: On one hand, the school should improve its maintenance of the system to lower the possibility of future mistakes; on the other hand, the school should take precautions to strengthen its self-protection. For instance, the school might mention in the offer that the offer will only become a valid legal document when the student responds to it; some other schools have the rule that an offer is only valid once the student sends in a deposit.

Ellie: It seems that I have to read acceptance letters carefully in the future, especially tips and side notes that are mentioned.

Dad: I hope your dream comes true!

Ellie: I hope I won't have any more of these dreams!

 Growth Revelation

Integrity is the foundation of a society, and integrity is important to an individual, a company, and the society as a whole.

A school admission notice is a legal document in which the school agrees to accept the student's admission. It is the school's commitment to the student and should not be easily changed. An admission notice usually include a clear indication of the student's admission, the enrollment time, the grade, the tuitions, etc. Some admission notices also include some important tips. Students should strictly follow the requirements of the notice, otherwise they might find themselves in trouble.

Think and Consider

1. What kind of dream did Ellie have?

2. What is your understanding of what a school offer is?

3. What do you think should be included in a school admission offer?

第八章
黑色星期五

·导读·

　　黑色星期五，艾莉全家出动去逛街，尽管之前已有思想准备，但商场里人山人海的盛况还是让艾莉感到意外和吃惊。艾莉一边照顾在水池边奔跑玩耍的弟弟，一边惦记着去游戏厅玩，但一场意外让艾莉的愿望彻底化为泡影。黑色星期五到底发生了什么？孩子在商场里玩耍时受伤，谁应该对此承担责任？

　　艾莉家住在新泽西州北部一个宁静的小镇。离家5分钟车程有一个全州知名的大型购物商场，这个商场占地面积有7个足球场那么大，商品更是琳琅满目，每天都吸引着来自世界各地的游客和购物者。

　　一周前，爸爸妈妈告诉艾莉，下周五是黑色星期五，商场大促销，全家准备一起去逛商场，看看有没有合适的家具买几件。听到这个好消息，艾莉狠狠地攥了一下拳头。要知道艾莉家搬到这里好几年了，艾莉还没见识过传说中的黑色星期五商场抢购的壮观景象呢！

　　尽管来之前艾莉已有思想准备，但黑色星期五的盛况还是超出了她的想象。以前只是在电视上看到过，现在艾莉才真正体会到什么叫"人山人海"了。不管是门店里面还是外面的过道上，商场的每一个角落都挤满了游客和购物者，黑压压一片。平时，商场里还会播放一些舒缓的轻音乐，但今天播放的全都是快节奏的音乐。人们根本无法停下脚步，因为一旦停下来就会影响其他人赶路或选购，弄得艾莉一时无处藏身。

刚刚和爸爸妈妈逛了一会儿，艾莉就觉得喘不过气来，逛街的兴趣顿时锐减。看到艾莉和弟弟一脸的无精打采，妈妈说："艾莉，这样吧，我和爸爸先去逛逛家具店，你带着弟弟到喷泉那边去玩，过一会儿我带你们去游戏厅。不过，今天哥哥不在，你要照看好弟弟！"

听到"游戏厅"几个字，艾莉和弟弟的眼睛不约而同地亮了起来，要知道游戏厅可是姐弟俩共同的最爱。

"好的，没问题！"艾莉满口答应。

"好久没打游戏了，今天我要好好过把瘾！"看着弟弟在喷泉边玩耍，艾莉忍不住地想。

商场的中央有个圆形的喷泉，喷泉中间有一个大大的滚动的玻璃球。喷泉上方是圆形穹顶，阳光透过穹顶的彩色玻璃洒下来，照在玻璃球上，晶莹剔透。不少游客在此驻足，或观赏，或拍照，更有游客站在池边向圆球中心投掷硬币，据说若能将钱币投到球里，就能获得好运。哗哗的流水声更是吸引了很多孩子，有些孩子在池边玩水，有些孩子围着水池奔跑，相互追逐。

弟弟也加入了奔跑追逐的行列。因为有些孩子玩水，水溅到了地面上，加上来来往往踩踏的人比较多，导致地面有些湿滑。因此，艾莉一直跟在弟弟的后面，照看着弟弟，生怕他滑倒。

跑了几圈之后，艾莉已是气喘吁吁，可是弟弟玩兴正浓，而且还吐着舌头挑衅："姐姐，你抓不到我，你抓不到我，咯咯咯，咯咯咯……"

这套激将法要是放在平时，艾莉肯定不会理会，但是今天却不一样。妈妈好不容易同意她去游戏厅"过瘾"，而且今天哥哥还没来，所以不管怎么样，一定要照顾好弟弟！艾莉心里暗暗地打定主意。

又跑了一会，艾莉实在跑不动了，弟弟也是满头大汗。

"你别乱跑，待在这儿，姐姐去给你买可乐。我们休息休息，过会儿再玩，好不好？"

可乐可是弟弟平时最喜欢喝的饮料，艾莉这招果然管用，调皮的弟弟一下子安静下来，郑重地点了点头："好的，但是你一定要给我买大杯哦！"

看到小家伙一脸严肃的样子，艾莉忍不住笑了："姐姐今天高兴，大杯就大杯！"

商店里买饮料的人排着长队，好不容易才排到了艾莉。买完单，拿着两大杯可乐，艾莉赶紧往回走，远远地看到弟弟正站在原地等着她。一看到姐姐手里拿着自己的"最爱"，弟弟张大嘴巴,迫不及待地向艾莉跑来。

"站住,别动!"艾莉高声叫道。

可是,弟弟似乎没听到,张着双臂继续向前奔跑。突然,弟弟脚下一滑,重重地摔倒在地上。艾莉一惊,手上的可乐险些掉在地上,几秒钟之后,传来弟弟痛苦的叫声。

艾莉三步并做两步地冲到弟弟身边,急切地问:"怎么样?你还好吧?还好吧?"

弟弟蜷缩在地上,双眼紧闭,眉头紧锁,表情极度痛苦,看起来伤得不轻。艾莉急得气都喘不过来,她努力让自己平静下来,一边安慰弟弟,一边赶紧给爸爸妈妈和急救中心打电话。爸爸妈妈闻讯赶到,过了一会儿,救护车也赶到了。

原本令人期待的周末就这样结束了,游戏厅也没去成,乐极生悲,真是个"黑色"星期五!

爸爸妈妈带着弟弟检查、拍片,忙个不停,艾莉一个人坐在医院走廊的长椅上,不停地责怪自己。不知道过了多久,妈妈走了过来。

艾莉急忙迎上去问:"弟弟的腿怎么样了?检查结果出来了吗?"

"诊断出来了,医生说是骨折,需要手术。"妈妈无奈地摇了摇头。

艾莉趴在妈妈肩上难过地哭了起来:"都怪我没照顾好弟弟,都怪我……"艾莉呜咽地重复着。

"也不能全怪你，商场里今天人多，水池里的水溅到地上，地面湿滑，工作人员没来得及清理。"妈妈安慰道。

"还是怪我，要是我不去买饮料就好了！"艾莉抽泣着。

"别难过了，你跟着邻居先回家，我和爸爸今晚留在这里照顾弟弟，明天我还要和商场联系后续事宜。"

第二天中午，爸爸从医院回到家，告诉艾莉弟弟已经做了手术，一切都还顺利，不过要住院一段时间。午饭后，艾莉和爸爸聊了起来。

艾莉：爸爸，我现在很纠结，昨天晚上都没怎么睡好。

爸爸：你纠结什么呢？

艾莉：一方面，我希望商场能够承担弟弟的医药费，毕竟手术和住院费用不菲；另一方面，我又觉得商场似乎不应该承担法律责任。

爸爸：嗯！看来我要努力工作，多赚点加班费，否则今年暑假的欧洲行就要变成国内游了。

艾莉：真的吗？可是我们去意大利的机票都订好了！

爸爸：别急，也没那么悲观！说说你的理由。

艾莉：我们逛商场完全是自愿的。虽然弟弟滑倒的主要原因是商场地面湿滑，但是地面湿滑是因为其他小朋友玩水溅到了地面上，不是因为水池漏水等商场设施的原因导致的。另外，如果我不去买饮料，一直跟着弟弟，他可能就不会滑倒受伤。

爸爸：听起来似乎有些道理。

艾莉：啊？不，我希望法官不这么认为！

爸爸：首先我们要弄清楚，商场有没有义务和责任保证顾客的安全？

艾莉：我不确定商场有没有这个义务，同时也不确定商场能不能承担得了这个义务。

爸爸：很好的问题！那么，商场是一个什么性质的场所？

艾莉：它和我们家不一样，我们家是私人领地。

爸爸：对的，商场是个公共场所。

艾莉：我们镇上的公园也是公共场所。

爸爸：都是公共场所，二者有什么不同吗？

艾莉：开商场是为了赚钱，公园是免费供市民休息的。

爸爸：对，商场是以赚钱为目的的经营性的公共场所。

艾莉："以赚钱为目的""经营性的"，看来这点很重要！我脑子似乎清楚一些了。

爸爸：很多商场都窗明几净、环境舒适，商家这么做的目的是什么呢？

艾莉：当然是为了吸引顾客来购物了！

爸爸：其实，从你走进商场大门的那一刻起，你和商场之间的交易行为就开始了。

艾莉：这个我有点不懂。

爸爸：想象一下你和妈妈到商场买衣服的过程。

艾莉：进商场、挑选、试穿、付款、包装、带走，基本上是这样的过程。

爸爸：这是成交的过程，也可能最后没成交。

艾莉：那是当然，我经常试了很多件衣服，最后一件都没买。

爸爸：购物从结果上看是"成交"或者"没成交"，但其实商家提供的是一个服务的过程。

艾莉：有点明白了，能继续解释一下吗？

爸爸：这个服务的过程就包括提供一个合适的交易场所。

艾莉：这是商家的义务？

爸爸：对，而且是非常重要的一部分义务！

艾莉：看来，商家要提供的并不仅仅是合格的商品那么简单。

爸爸：商家既要给顾客提供合格的商品，还要提供合适的交易场所。

艾莉：那么，什么样的场所是合适的交易场所呢？

爸爸：这个似乎很难规定一个统一的标准。事实上，商场为了吸引顾客，手段可谓层出不穷，商场一个比一个大，装修一个比一个豪华。

艾莉：那有没有一个最基本的要求呢？

爸爸：商场作为面向公众的经营性场所，法律对它最基本的要求就是"安全"！

艾莉：这下我明白了，如果商场场地不安全，即使它有再好的商品也不能营业。

爸爸：想想看，如果商场不能保证自己的交易场所是安全的，那会怎么样？

艾莉：我肯定不敢去商场购物了。

爸爸：或者大家都穿着铠甲或者戴着头盔逛商场？

艾莉：哈哈，那太搞笑了，商场变成战场了！

爸爸：还没那么严重。

艾莉：我只是开个玩笑。

爸爸：所以，商场首先要保证顾客的人身安全。

艾莉：这个我同意，毕竟没有什么比人的生命和健康更重要了。

爸爸：还是那句老话，安全第一！

艾莉：我理解了。以前在电视里看到，商场电梯失控或者悬挂的广告牌掉下来导致顾客受伤，商场都要对受伤的顾客承担赔偿责任，就是因为商场没有履行好保证顾客人身安全的义务。

爸爸：事实上，商场是公共场所，涉及公共安全，因此，很多国家和地区的法律对商场的物业面积、承力、结构、通风、装修等都有明确的要求，而且商场还要经过相关政府部门验收合格后才能开业。

艾莉：看来经营商场不是一件容易的事。不过，我记得以前您讲过，承担法律责任的前提条件是当事人要有过错。

爸爸：是，这点很重要，看来你已经记住了！

艾莉：耶！给自己点个赞！

爸爸：虽然法律规定商场有义务保证交易场所的安全，但是如果商场没有过错，即使顾客有损害发生，商场也不必承担责任。

艾莉：能举些商场没有过错的例子吗？

爸爸：比如，一个人想自杀，从商场楼上跳下来，导致身亡；再比如，两个人在商场里打架，导致其中一人受伤，等等。

艾莉：明白了，第一个损害的发生是当事人自身的原因导致的，而第二个损害是由第三方原因导致的。

爸爸：对，在上述两种情况下，商场都没有过错，所以商场对此不必承担法律责任。

艾莉：那么，怎么判断商场是否有过错呢？

爸爸：主要是看商场是否尽到了其应尽的义务。

艾莉：那这次商场尽到了它应尽的义务了吗？

爸爸：你觉得呢？

艾莉：我还是有点犹豫。一方面，弟弟受伤肯定不是他自己或者我们愿意看到的，也不是由第三方导致的；另一方面，黑色星期五商场里的人太多，清洁工可能确实忙不过来，没能及时清理地上的积水。

爸爸：我们再仔细讨论一下细节。

艾莉：好的，魔鬼都在细节里！

爸爸：首先，商场应不应该知道水池里的水会溅出来，溅出的水会导致地面湿滑，地面湿滑可能会导致行人摔倒？

艾莉：这个他们肯定知道。

爸爸：为什么这么确定？

艾莉：以前逛商场的时候，我见过商场工作人员在水池附近拖地，清理溅出来的水。

爸爸：我也见过。

艾莉：这说明商场知道水池里的水会溅到地面上，而且那天商场还在水池边竖了一块牌子，上面写着"地面湿滑，注意安全"。

爸爸：这么说，商场也知道地面湿滑可能会导致危险？

艾莉：对。

爸爸：那么，商场采取什么必要的措施了吗？

艾莉：那天我和弟弟在水池边玩了近一个小时，没见到商场工作人员过来打扫地面。

爸爸：可能是黑色星期五生意太好，人手忙不过来？或者是还没到打扫的时间？

艾莉：人手忙不过来能成为免除责任的理由吗？

爸爸：你觉得呢？

艾莉：我觉得不能。既然开了商场，商家就应该有能力应对这种情况，人手不够就应该增加人手，否则就不要开门营业。

爸爸：不过，增加人手可能导致商场经营成本增加、利润减少。

艾莉：但是,商场不能为了降低成本或者为了赚更多的钱,就不顾顾客的安全啊,安全是第一位的!

爸爸：同意。

艾莉：而且,商场知道黑色星期五人会很多,应该采取更多、更有力的措施,保证商场的安全。

爸爸：商家不是立了警示牌了吗?

艾莉：我觉得这还不够!警示牌不是每个人都能看到的,而且有些年龄小的小朋友也未必看得懂。

爸爸：你觉得商场还可以采取一些什么样的防护措施呢?

艾莉：比如,增加打扫地面的次数,平时每小时打扫一次,黑色星期五可以每半小时或者15分钟打扫一次;再比如,可以在水池外面增加一道护栏,这样小朋友就到不了水池边了。

爸爸：看来其他有效的方法还是有的。

艾莉：有!而且这些措施都是商家完全可以做到的。我记得有些公共场所或者公共设施,在遇到紧急情况时甚至会临时关闭,就是为了防止由于人多而导致伤害的发生。

爸爸：商场明知道水池里的水溅出会导致地面湿滑,而地面湿滑可能导致行人受伤,同时商场也有能力采取更多的措施保证商场的安全,但是商场没有这么做,所以,它没有尽到应尽的管理义务。换句话说,商场有过错,所以它应该对弟弟的受伤承担法律责任。

艾莉：太好了！这么一讨论，我心里一下子亮堂了很多。

爸爸：可是，我感觉你还是没有完全放松下来。

艾莉：您知道原因的。

爸爸：我知道！你自己去买饮料，丢下弟弟一个人在水池边玩，你很内疚，觉得自己也有责任，对吧？

艾莉：弟弟只有5岁，还不完全知道什么是危险，如果我一直跟着他，他可能就不会摔倒。

爸爸：有可能。不过地面确实很湿滑，即使你在，弟弟跑来跑去，也可能会摔倒。据说那天摔倒了好几个人。

艾莉：但是如果我在，至少弟弟摔倒的可能性会小一些。

爸爸：看来，商场没有尽到应尽的管理义务，你也没有照看好弟弟，这两个因素共同导致了损害的发生。

艾莉：是。不过，我认为主要责任还是在商场，我负次要责任。

爸爸：我同意。

艾莉：所以，去意大利的旅行还是如期进行，但是我原计划买的衣服就不买了，呜呜！

爸爸：我和妈妈也有些责任，我们应该知道水池附近危险，所以当时应该提醒你注意安全。而且，你也是孩子，在那种情况下，我们不应该把照顾弟弟的任务完全交给你。所以，意大利之行如期进行，但是原计划我要买的皮鞋就不买了，呜呜！

艾莉：现在我心情好多了！

爸爸：就讨论到这吧，我去医院看看你妈妈和商场沟通得怎么样了。

艾莉：好的，我在家等着你们的好消息！

·成长启示·

商场作为一个经营性的场所，应该保证其场地和设施安全好用，不会给进入商场的顾客造成伤害，这是商场的基本义务。

如果商场明知道其经营场地或设施可能导致损害，但是没有采取有效的措施，则商场应该对由此导致的损害承担责任。但是，如果商场已经尽到了管理义务，则即使有损害发生，它也不必承担法律责任。

商场是个公共场所，人多杂乱，家长带孩子逛商场时应该照顾好自己的孩子。

·成长思考·

1. 弟弟为什么会滑倒？
2. 你觉得商场是一个什么样的场所？
3. 你觉得怎样才能减少或者避免小朋友在商场里玩耍时受伤？

Chapter 8

Black Friday

📖 Reading Guide

On Black Friday, Ellie's family went shopping. Although Ellie expected a large crowd, the number of people in the mall still surprised her. While watching her brother as he ran around the fountain in the mall, Ellie couldn't stop thinking about going to the arcade. An accident, however, crushed Ellie's wish. What happened on Black Friday? When children get injured running around a mall, who should be held responsible?

Ellie lived in a quiet town in northern New Jersey. Five minutes away from her house was a well-known, large shopping mall. The shopping mall was huge (approximately equivalent to 7 soccer fields!) and was home to a number of wonderful stores enticing shoppers from around the world every day.

A week before, Mom and Dad told Ellie that the next Friday would be "Black Friday" — the day when many stores would hold huge sales. Ellie's family wanted to take advantage of these sales to possibly buy additional furniture for their home. Hearing this good news, Ellie was excited: her family moved to their current home several years ago, but this was going to be her first time witnessing the legendary spectacle of Black Friday!

Although Ellie had been mentally prepared for the scene, Black Friday was beyond her imagination. She had seen footage of Black Friday on the evening news before but witnessing it in person had renewed her definition of "crowded." Whether they were inside the stores or outside walking through the halls, every corner of the mall was crowded with eager shoppers. On a normal day, the mall played soothing, light music in the background, but today, all the music that Ellie heard were fast-paced songs designed to encourage people to keep moving. It was so fast-paced that Ellie felt like she could not slow down or else she would be lost in the crowd!

After shopping for a while with her parents, Ellie and her brother began to feel breathless and lost interest in going into more stores. Seeing Ellie and her brother's emotionless faces, Mom said, "Ellie, here's the plan. Your father and I are going to the furniture store first. You can take your brother to the fountain to take a break. After a while, I will take you to the arcade. Now remember, because your older brother did not come with us, you have to look after your younger brother!"

Hearing the word "arcade," Ellie and her brother's eyes lit up in unison: the arcade was their favorite place to visit.

"OK, no problem!" Ellie promised.

"It has been a while since I went to the arcade last time, and I am going to have all the fun I can today!" Watching her brother as he ran around the fountain, Ellie could not stop herself from thinking about it.

There was a circular fountain in the center of the mall with a big glass ball in the middle of the fountain. Above the fountain was a round dome, where the sun shone through the stained glass and onto the glass ball, reflecting the colorful light in many directions. Many tourists stopped there to watch or take pictures, and others stood at the side of pool and aimed to throw coins into the ball. It was said that if you could toss the coins into the ball, you would have good fortune. The sound of flowing water attracted many children. Some played with water by the fountain, while others ran around the fountain and chased each other.

Ellie's younger brother soon joined other children in a game of running and chasing around the fountain. Because some children were playing with water, water was splashed on the ground, and Ellie followed her brother around so that she could look after him, fearing that he would slip and fall.

After running a few laps around the fountain, Ellie was

feeling tired while her younger brother was just getting started. He stuck out his tongue to provoke Ellie, "Ellie, you can't catch me, you can't catch me, blah blah blah!"

Usually, this kind of goading would not affect Ellie at all, but it was different today. Mom finally agreed to take her to the arcade, and today, her older brother did not come, so no matter what, she had to take good care of her younger brother! Ellie quietly hatched a plan ...

After running for a while, her brother was sweating as well, prompting Ellie to say, "Don't go anywhere. Stay here, and I am going to buy you a Coke. We will take a break from playing, and we can join the other kids later, OK?"

Coke was her brother's favorite drink. Ellie's trick worked. Her naughty brother calmed down immediately and solemnly nodded, "OK, but you must buy me a large one!"

Seeing the little guy looking so serious, Ellie couldn't help herself from smiling, "OK, I'm in a good mood today."

There was a long line for sodas, and it took a while for Ellie to get to the front of the line. Ellie hurried back with the drinks and saw that her brother was standing in the same place, waiting for her. As soon as he saw his sister holding his favorite drink, her brother opened his mouth and didn't hesitate to run to Ellie.

"Stand there. Don't move!" Ellie yelled.

However, the younger brother did not seem to have heard her. He continued to run toward her with his arms flung open. Suddenly, her younger brother slipped and fell to the ground. Ellie was shocked. The soda in her hands almost fell to the ground. A few seconds later, the sound of her brother's painful cry echoed in the aisle.

Ellie rushed to her brother in large steps and eagerly asked, "How are you feeling? Are you okay? Are you fine?"

The younger brother curled up on the ground with his eyes closed and his brows locked. Ellie was so anxious that she couldn't breathe. She tried to calm herself down and comfort her brother while calling her parents and the emergency center. When Mom and Dad heard the news, they rushed to the fountain where, not long after, they were joined by the paramedics.

A day originally intended to be full of fun ultimately ended on a bad note. Everyone was upset, and no one went to the arcade. What a "Black" Friday!

Ellie's parents accompanied her younger brother to the hospital and were busy for the rest of the day as he underwent X-rays. Ellie sat alone on a hospital bench in the waiting room, blaming herself for her brother's injury. She waited for a long time before her mom walked toward her.

Ellie hurried up to her mother and asked, "How is my

brother? Do we have the results?"

"The doctor said that it is a very bad fracture and that he needs to be hospitalized in preparation for surgery," Mom shook her head helplessly.

Out of sorrow, Ellie cried on her mother's shoulder, "It was all my fault! I did not take good care of my brother. It was all because of me ..." Ellie repeated in a sob.

"It was not purely your fault. There were so many people in the mall today. The water in the fountain splashed onto the ground, making it slippery, and the staff didn't have time to clean it up," Mom comforted her.

"It was still my fault! If I had not left to buy soda for him, everything would have been fine!" Ellie sobbed.

"Don't be sad. Our neighbor is going to come take you home while your father and I will stay here to take care of your brother. I will contact the mall tomorrow for follow-up."

At noon on the next day, Dad came home from the hospital and told Ellie that her brother had an operation during the night. Everything went well, but he had to stay in the hospital for a while. After lunch, Ellie started to chat with her father.

Ellie: Dad, I am struggling emotionally right now. I didn't sleep well last night.

Dad: What are you struggling with?

Ellie: On one hand, I hope that the mall can afford the medical expenses for my brother. After all, the surgery and hospitalization are expensive; on the other hand, I feel that the mall does not seem to bear legal responsibility for the incident.

Dad: Sounds reasonable! It seems that I have to work hard and earn more overtime pay this year. Otherwise, we would not be able to travel outside of the country this year for vacation.

Ellie: Really? But we already booked our tickets to Italy!

Dad: Don't worry. Don't be so pessimistic. What are your reasons for thinking that the mall does not bear legal responsibility?

Ellie: First, it was completely our decision to go to the mall. Additionally, the main reason that my brother slipped was that the ground was slippery as a result of other children splashing water on the ground — not because of water leaking from the fountain. Finally, if I hadn't left to go buy a drink for my brother and had kept an eye on him, he may not have slipped and hurt himself.

Dad: It sounds somewhat reasonable.

Ellie: Really? I really hope the judge doesn't feel that way!

Dad: First of all, we have to figure out whether the mall has the obligation and responsibility to ensure the safety of its customers.

Ellie: I am not sure if the mall is obligated to do so, and I am also not sure whether the mall can bear this duty.

Dad: This is a good point! So, what kind of place is the mall?

Ellie: It is different from our house. Our house is a private property.

Dad: Yes, the mall is a public place.

Ellie: The park in our town is also a public place.

Dad: They are both public places. What is different between a mall and a park?

Ellie: Malls are open to sell products and make money, while the park is free for the citizens of the town to go to and relax at.

Dad: Yes, the mall is a business-oriented public place for the purpose of making money.

Ellie: "For the purpose of making money," "business-oriented": it seems that these are key words! I seem to understand the situation a little more.

Dad: Many shopping malls have clean windows and a comfortable environment. What is the purpose of keeping them this way?

Ellie: It is obviously for the purpose of attracting customers to shop!

Dad: Actually, from the moment you walk into the mall, the contract between you and the mall is in effect.

Ellie: You lost me.

Dad: Imagine the sequence of events when your mother goes to the mall to buy clothes.

Ellie: Entering the mall, picking the clothes, trying them on, paying, packing, and taking the clothes — that's basically what she does.

Dad: Correct — that is the general sequence for a successful transaction. There is also the possibility that a transaction is not completed in the end.

Ellie: Of course, I often try on a lot of clothes but end up not buying anything.

Dad: Looking at the results of shopping, it is usually either "deal" or "no deal," but in fact, the shops provides a service process.

Ellie: I kind of understand it now, but can you explain further?

Dad: The process of this service includes providing a suitable trading venue — a place that is comfortable and entices people to purchase goods.

Ellie: Is this a business obligation?

Dad: Yes, and it is a very important part of the shop's obligations!

Ellie: It seems that a shop owner needs to provide more than just qualified products.

Dad: Shop owners must provide not only qualified products but also suitable trading venues to customers.

Ellie: So, what kind of places are considered to be "suitable trading venues"?

Dad: It can be difficult to standardize that. In fact, in order to attract customers, the malls have endless possible ways and methods. The malls usually get grander and grander, and the decorations get more luxurious than the ones before.

Ellie: Then, is there some kind of basic requirement?

Dad: Malls are a business-oriented places for the public. The most basic requirement, according to the law, is "safety"!

Ellie: I understand that! If a mall is not safe, even if it has the best products, it can't be open to the public.

Dad: Think about it. What would happen if a mall can't guarantee that its trading venue is safe?

Ellie: I definitely won't want to go shopping at that mall.

Dad: Or maybe everyone would wear armor and helmets to go to the mall?

Ellie: Ha-ha, that would be funny! The mall would become a battlefield!

Dad: I don't think the situation will escalate to that level yet.

Ellie: I'm just joking.

Dad: So, the stores must first guarantee the personal safety of their customers.

Ellie: I agree. After all, nothing is more important than a person's life and health.

Dad: Just like the proverb says: safety first!

Ellie: I understand. I had seen on TV events where the elevators in a mall were out of control or where the advertisement placards fell to the floor, causing customers to be injured. The shopping malls were responsible for the injured customers because the malls did not fulfill their obligations to ensure the personal safety of the customers.

Dad: In fact, because malls are public spaces and thus involve the safety of the general public, many countries and regions have clear requirements about the property area, capacity, structure, ventilation, decoration, etc. of malls, and they must be approved by the relevant government departments before they can start business.

Ellie: It seems that operating a mall is not an easy task. However, I remember that you said before that the prerequisite for legal liability is that the party in question must be proven to be at fault.

Dad: Yes, this is very important, and it seems like that you already remembered!

Ellie: Yeah! A big thumbs up for me!

Dad: Although the law stipulates that the mall has the obligation to ensure the safety of the trading venue, if the mall is not at fault, then it does not have to bear the responsibility even if the customer was harmed.

Ellie: Can you give some examples of when the malls are not fault?

Dad: For example, when a person who wants to commit suicide jumps off from the top of the mall, causing death, the mall would not be at fault. Another example would be the situation where two people fight in the mall, causing one of them to be injured. There are many more examples.

Ellie: I understand. The first damage occurred because of the person's own choices and decisions, and the second damage was caused by a third party.

Dad: Yes, in both cases, the mall was not at fault, so the mall does not have to bear legal responsibility for those situations.

Ellie: So, how do you judge whether a mall is at fault?

Dad: It is mainly determined by whether the mall has fulfilled its due obligations.

Ellie: In our case, did the mall fulfill its obligations?

Dad: What do you think?

Ellie: I am still a little hesitant. On one hand, my brother's injury was definitely not planned by him, nor were we willing to witness it happen, and nor was it caused by a third party. On the other hand, there were too many people in mall on Black Friday. The cleaners might have been busy, so they were not able to clean up the water on the ground in time.

Dad: Let's discuss the details carefully.

Ellie: OK, the truth is often in the details!

Dad: First of all, should the mall have been aware of the fact that the water from the fountain could possibly spill out, which would cause the floor to be slippery, further causing costumers to slip and fall?

Ellie: They definitely knew about this.

Dad: Why are you so sure?

Ellie: In the past, I have seen mall staff mopping the floor near the fountain to clean up the splashed water.

Dad: I have seen that as well.

Ellie: This shows that the mall knew that the water in the fountain could splash on the ground. In addition, the mall also placed a sign near the fountain that day, with the words "Caution — Wet Floor!" on it.

Dad: So, the mall knew that the ground being slippery could potentially cause injuries?

Ellie: Right.

Dad: So, what were some necessary measures that the mall took?

Ellie: I played with my brother for nearly an hour at the fountain that day and during that time I didn't see the mall staff coming over to mop up the water.

Dad: Maybe Black Friday was a busy day for them, so they didn't have enough janitors for the mall? Or maybe it wasn't time to clean up yet?

Ellie: Is "too busy" a justified excuse for the accident?

Dad: What do you think?

Ellie: I don't think it is. Since the mall had opened, they should have been able to cope with this situation. If there had not been enough people, they should have hired more people. Otherwise, they should not have even been in business.

Dad: However, increasing the number of employees might lead to increased operating costs and reduced profits.

Ellie: However, a mall can't ignore the safety of customers in order to cut costs or make more money. Safety comes first!

Dad: Correct.

Ellie: Furthermore, the mall knew that there would be a lot of people on Black Friday, so they should have taken more measures and more efficient ones to ensure the safety of the costumers.

Dad: Didn't the mall put up a sign that warned you of the floor?

Ellie: I don't think that was enough! The warning signs were not visible to everyone, and some younger children even may not have been able to understand them.

Dad: What other kinds of protective measures do you think the mall could have taken?

Ellie: For example, they should have increased the number of times that they cleaned the floor. For example, I think that it is usually cleaned once an hour. On Black Friday, knowing how busy the mall will be, the floor could have been cleaned every half-hour or even every fifteen minutes. Another example is that they could have added a guardrail around the fountain so that children would not have been able to come near the fountain.

Dad: It seems that there are effective ways to prevent accidents like this one.

Ellie: Yes! And these measures are completely achievable by the mall. I remember that some public facilities even temporarily closed in case of an emergency, just to prevent the occurrence of injuries due to a large number of people.

Dad: The mall knew that the water spilling out from the fountain would cause the ground to become slippery and that the slippery ground might cause pedestrians to be injured. At the same time, the mall had the ability to take more measures to ensure the safety of the customers, but the mall did not do so. So, the mall did not fulfill its management obligations. In other words, the mall was at fault, so it should be legally responsible for the injury of your younger brother.

Ellie: Great! After the discussion, my heart suddenly lightened a lot.

Dad: But I feel that you are still not completely relaxed.

Ellie: You know why.

Dad: I know exactly why! You went to buy a drink by yourself, leaving your brother alone to play around the fountain. You feel that you were also responsible for the accident. Am I right?

Ellie: My brother is only 5 years old, and he doesn't understand what is dangerous and what is not. If I had continued to look after him by following him, maybe he would not have tripped.

Dad: That is a possibility, but the ground was really slippery, and even if you were there, your brother may still have slipped and fallen. Apparently, several people fell that day.

Ellie: But if I had been there, my brother would have been less likely to fall.

Dad: It seems that the mall did not fulfill its management obligations, and you did not take good care of your younger brother. These two factors together caused the eventual damage.

Ellie: Yes. However, I think that the mall should take the major blame, and I bear the minor responsibility.

Dad: I agree.

Ellie: So, the trip to Italy is still going to be happen, but the clothes I originally planned to buy will not be a part of the plan. That's unfortunate!

Dad: Your mother and I also bear some responsibilities. We should have known about the dangers near the fountain, and we should have reminded you to pay more attention. Besides, you are also a child. In that case, we should not have given you the task of taking care of your brother. Therefore, the trip to Italy will be carried out as scheduled, but the leather shoes I originally planned to buy will no longer be a part of the plan. What a pity!

Ellie: Now I am in a better mood!

Dad: OK, let's stop here for now. I am going to the hospital to see your mother, who is communicating with the mall about this situation.

Ellie: OK, I will be waiting for your good news at home!

 Growth Revelation

As a business, a mall should ensure that its venues and facilities are safe and easy to use and will not cause harm to customers entering the mall. This is the basic obligation of a mall.

If a mall knows that its premises or facilities may cause damage but fails to take effective protective measures, the mall should be held liable for damage caused thereby. However, if the mall has fulfilled its management obligations, it will not have to bear legal responsibility, even if damage is caused.

Shopping malls are public facilities, with many visitors every day. Parents should take care of their children when they take their children shopping.

Think and Consider

1. Why did Ellie's brother slip and fall?

2. What kind of place do you think the mall is?

3. How do you think we can reduce or avoid the possibility of children getting injured while playing in the mall?

第九章

正当防卫

·导读·

艾莉和瑞安是学校击剑队的队友，下午训练后一起回家。路上遇到了校霸托尼，托尼动手殴打瑞安，瑞安还击并拿着棒球棒追打托尼，结果会怎么样呢？如果托尼受伤，瑞安要不要承担法律责任？

瑞安是新学年转来的新生。他一头卷发，面容清秀，身材不高，甚至有些瘦小，一双乌黑的大眼睛炯炯有神。瑞安从6岁就开始学习击剑，是击剑高手，因此入学没几天便成了学校击剑队的主力，而且已经有了不少粉丝。

艾莉一直在俱乐部练排球。由于学校没有排球队，所以进入八年级后，艾莉选择了学校的花剑项目。艾莉以前没有练过击剑，完全是新手，不过由于有运动基础，她进步得很快。瑞安也练花剑，经常给艾莉一些建议，帮助艾莉纠正技术动作。

一天下午放学，艾莉和队友们陆续来到训练馆，大家有说有笑，着手开始做准备活动。瑞安最后一个进来，重重地把包丢在地上，没有和任何人打招呼。分组对抗时，瑞安更是不在状态，连输了好几局，甚至输给了他以前从未输过的队友。瑞安今天是怎么了？艾莉心里嘀咕着。

训练课结束，大家互道再见，陆续离开了训练馆，只剩下艾莉和瑞安。

"瑞安，你今天状态不对呀，出什么事了吗？"艾莉关切地问。

"嗯……也没什么。"瑞安垂着头，语气中明显带着犹豫。

"如果需要什么帮助的话，你可以告诉我，我也许可以帮上忙。"艾莉热心地提议道。

犹豫了一下，瑞安终于开口问道："是托尼，你熟悉他吗？"

"知道，他是隔壁 B 学校有名的校霸，以前经常欺负其他同学，被学校警告过两次，据说上了 11 年级以后好了一些。怎么，他欺负你了？"艾莉问道。

"倒也没有。今天来训练馆的路上，我经过停车场的时候遇到了他。他从车上下来对我吼叫，让我离他的车远点，还让我以后听他的话，否则下次见面给我好看，还让我小心他的刀。"瑞安虽然看上去很平静，但艾莉还是能感觉到他的沮丧。

"这么过分，要不要找老师或者校长跟他的学校反映一下？"艾莉气愤地提议。

"我想先不用吧，也许他只是说说。况且我刚来，一点小事就向老师打小报告，影响也不好，我自己能解决。"瑞安说着，自信地仰了仰头。

"好吧，那你自己当心，也许真的没什么。"艾莉鼓励道。

接下来几天的训练，瑞安慢慢恢复了状态，找回了感觉，又开始所向披靡。星期四训练课结束，瑞安心情很好，因为今天的训练赛他都赢了。艾莉今天的成绩也不错，打了5场仅输了1场。

"前几天你帮我纠正后退动作很有效，我觉得今天我的后退防守很自如。"艾莉抓住时机向瑞安表示感谢。

"那可是我的看家本领，不轻易教给别人的！"瑞安说着，会意地笑了。

"放心吧，我绝不会教给其他同学的。"艾莉开玩笑道。"为了表示对你的感谢，我今天请你喝星巴克的火龙果果汁吧。"艾莉又说。

"好啊，正好我今天特别渴。"瑞安不客气地说。

艾莉和瑞安背着包，穿过停车场向星巴克走去。艾莉注意到，瑞安这几天背的包比以前的大很多。艾莉正要问时，远远地看到一个高大而又熟悉的身影迎面走来。

"是托尼，真是冤家路窄！"艾莉暗暗地想。

托尼显然也认出了瑞安，径直向他们俩走过来。

"臭小子，怎么又遇到你了！"托尼开口便骂骂咧咧，顺手推搡了瑞安一下，瑞安顺势一闪，托尼没打到。

瑞安的举动似乎激怒了托尼，托尼又打了一拳，这一拳瑞安没能躲开，重重地打在了瑞安的左肩上。瑞安一个趔趄，险些跌倒。托尼抡起拳头又向瑞安打去，瑞安双脚起跳后退一步，避开了托尼的拳头，然后猛地一记直拳，重重地打在了托尼的左脸上。托尼没有任何防备，忙用手捂住自己的左脸，瑞安顺势右手又一拳，打在了托尼的右脸上。

趁着托尼还没缓过神，瑞安转身便跑，边跑边喊："艾莉，快回家！"

托尼哪儿受过这样的"欺负"，他像一头发了疯的雄狮一样在瑞安后面紧追。毕竟托尼人高马大，没几步便追上了瑞安。托尼从后面按住了瑞安的脖子，把他压在了地上。

"托尼，住手，别打了，再打我叫警察了！"艾莉高声呼叫。

突然，艾莉发现托尼放开瑞安，转身往回跑，瑞安起身便追，而且手里还多了一根棒球棒。托尼跑到艾莉跟前时，脚下可能踩到了一块石头，一个趔趄，险些摔倒。瑞安正好赶到，举起棒子，重重地打了托尼一棒子。托尼一下子趴在地上，昏了过去，血顺着头顶流了下来。艾莉被眼前这突如其来的一幕吓呆了，嘴巴张得老大，半天也说不出话。瑞安显然也没料到这个结果，手里的木棒一下子掉在了地上。艾莉好不容易缓过神来，赶紧掏出电话，打电话给警察和叫救护车。瑞安从包里取出了一块毛巾，蹲下身，用毛巾按住了托尼的伤口。过了一会儿，警察和救护车赶到，医护人员迅速地把托尼抬上救护车，直奔医院而去。

警察问:"这是怎么回事?"

"是我，是我打的。"瑞安声音有些颤抖。

"那你呢?"警察问艾莉。

"我是他同学，我们放学一起回家。"艾莉小声回答道。

"这样吧，瑞安跟我回警察局配合调查，时间挺晚了，艾莉留个电话，如果有需要的话，我们再跟你和你的家长联系。"警察说道。

看到瑞安上了警察的车，艾莉一路狂奔跑回了家。正好爸爸妈妈都在，艾莉上气不接下气地把刚才发生的事情告诉了爸爸妈妈。

看到艾莉身体不停地发抖，妈妈赶紧把她抱在怀里。"没事了，孩子，没事了，都会好起来的!"妈妈不停地安慰艾莉。

第二天刚到学校，艾莉便被叫到了校长办公室，昨天处理现场的警察也在校长办公室。

艾莉详细地把事情的经过说了一遍后，警察问:"瑞安之前有没有跟你说过他包里有一根棒球棒?"

艾莉回想了一下，说:"没有，他没和我说过。前几天他只是说托尼威胁过他，我还让他当心点。"

"瑞安用棒子打托尼时，托尼有没有攻击瑞安?"警察继续问道。

艾莉沉默了一会儿，说:"当时托尼在逃跑，好像脚底滑了一下，差点摔倒，所以没有攻击瑞安。"

"瑞安有没有说他为什么要追打托尼？"警察追问道。

"看到托尼出了很多血，我当时吓坏了，问瑞安为什么打得这么重，瑞安说托尼要到车上去取刀，所以……"艾莉喃喃道。

"好的，我没有问题了，你上课去吧。"警察说道。

"瑞安怎么样了？"看到警察准备要走，艾莉急切地问。

"瑞安今天上午还要继续配合调查，估计下午能回来上课。"警察说完，起身离开了校长办公室。

艾莉一整天情绪都很低落。

晚饭时，爸爸告诉艾莉，他刚和校长通过电话，校长说托尼已经确诊为中度脑震荡，需要住院治疗，不过应该没有什么生命危险。艾莉忍不住和爸爸探讨起这件事。

艾莉：爸爸，您觉得瑞安的行为是不是正当防卫？

爸爸：你这问题单刀直入啊！

艾莉：我上网查过了！

爸爸：网上怎么说？

艾莉：网上说，对正在实施不法侵害行为的人采取制止的措施，造成不法侵害人一定限度损害的，属于正当防卫，防卫人无须承担法律责任。也就是说，如果瑞安的行为构成正当防卫，那么瑞安就无须承担法律责任。

爸爸：让我们来看看事情的起因吧。

艾莉：起因是放学的路上，托尼截住我们，动手殴打瑞安。

爸爸：是谁先动手的？

艾莉：当然是托尼了，他先推搡了瑞安，后来又重重打了瑞安一拳。

爸爸：看来是托尼的过错在先。

艾莉：他之前就威胁过瑞安。

爸爸：托尼的行为是什么行为？

艾莉：肯定是错误的行为！

爸爸：除非是为了执行公务等法定原因，否则任何人都无权侵害他人的身体。托尼的行为是不法侵害他人身体的行为，他的行为损害和威胁了瑞安的健康和安全。

艾莉：执行公务？法定原因？能举个例子吗？

爸爸：比如，警察追捕逃犯，开枪射击。

艾莉：那我们之前讨论的溺水救人的事件中，利奥打了欧文一拳，是紧急避险，这也算是法定原因吧？

爸爸：对，这是在紧急情况下为了避免自己或者他人利益受损或者避免损失扩大而采取的行为，属于法定原因。在有法定原因的情况下，即使造成了他人的损害，行为人也无须承担法律责任。

艾莉：哈哈，给自己点个赞！

爸爸：正当防卫要求不法侵害行为是客观存在的，不能是想象侵害。

艾莉：还有想象的侵害吗？

爸爸：比如，你提到托尼以前曾经威胁过瑞安，见面时如果托尼并没有打瑞安，但是瑞安误以为托尼要伤害他，这就是想象中的伤害，事实上伤害并不存在。

艾莉：明白了，在这种情况下，如果瑞安出手打了托尼就不是正当防卫。

爸爸：当时瑞安有没有还手？

艾莉：有，托尼打了瑞安之后，瑞安出手还击。

爸爸：瑞安出手还击是为了制止托尼的不法侵害，是为了保护自己，是一种防卫行为。

艾莉：这个法律应该保护吧？法律总不会规定人们挨打还不能还手吧？

爸爸：那是当然，保护自己的安全是人们最基本的权利。

艾莉：这个我同意，面对不法侵害人，法律不仅要鼓励人们积极对抗，而且还要鼓励人们帮助他人对付坏人。

爸爸：正当防卫要求不法侵害行为正在发生，如果侵害行为尚未发生或者已经结束了，再去实施伤害行为就不能构成正当防卫。

艾莉：能举个例子吗？

爸爸：比如，托尼打了瑞安一拳后没再继续追打，他们各自回家了，瑞安越想越生气，拿着棒球棒找到托尼，打伤了托尼。

艾莉：这是报复。

爸爸：你觉得法律应该鼓励或保护这种报复行为吗？

艾莉：不应该，毕竟这样会造成新的伤害。

爸爸：对，法律不鼓励"以暴制暴"！

艾莉：不过，被人欺负的感觉确实很不好，有时心中怒气难消。

爸爸：不用急，法律会惩罚这些欺负别人的人。

艾莉：那么，这次的情况应该是不法侵害正在进行吧？

爸爸：当时托尼追打瑞安，后来为什么托尼突然又逃跑了？

艾莉：瑞安从包里拿出了棒球棒，托尼害怕了，所以转身逃跑。

爸爸：那是不是可以认为，托尼当时的侵害行为已经结束了呢？

艾莉：呃，我似乎中了您的圈套！

爸爸：我不是故意的！

艾莉：不过，当时我们都吓傻了，根本不知道托尼还会不会再次伤害瑞安。瑞安后来说，他以为托尼逃跑是想到车上取刀子。

爸爸：也就是说，瑞安很难准确判断伤害是否已经结束？

艾莉：不是难，是根本做不到。我们也不知道托尼要干什么，也许他真是去找刀呢。您知道吗，托尼以前经常欺负同学，平时我们都怕他。

爸爸：看来当时托尼的伤害还没有完全消除，还有伤害的可能。

艾莉：看来您真不是故意的，给您也点个赞！

爸爸：你觉不觉得瑞安下手有点重？

艾莉：圈套又来了！我知道您想说瑞安的防卫行为是不是过当。

爸爸：对，即使你的行为是正当防卫行为，但如果超过了必要的限度，就构成了防卫过当，也要承担一定的法律责任。

艾莉：这对防卫者要求很高啊！

爸爸：想想看，为什么要有这样的要求呢？

艾莉：正当防卫虽然是为了保护自己或者他人免受伤害，但是可能会导致施害者受到伤害。

爸爸：是的。正当防卫虽然制止了施害人的不法行为，但是有时会给施害者造成一些伤害，因此，它具有一定的"以暴制暴"的性质。如果不对防卫的程度加以限制，放任防卫人的行为，对施害人也不公平。

艾莉：那么，怎么判断防卫有没有超过必要的限度呢？

爸爸：这个很复杂，要结合当时的具体情况。

艾莉：有没有什么标准呢？

爸爸：一般情况下，如果防卫行为明显超过了必要的限度并且造成了严重的后果，便构成防卫过当。也就是说，为了制止某种不法行为，明显不用采取那么过激的措施，如果防卫人采取了，可能会被认为"明显超过必要的限度"。

艾莉：就是说"杀鸡不用宰牛刀"？

爸爸：有点这个意思。比如，别人打了你一个耳光，你没有必要拿出一个大砍刀来防卫。

艾莉：明白，打一个耳光仅是皮肉之苦，大砍刀可能会砍死人的，确实过了！

爸爸：那么，为了制止托尼的伤害，瑞安拿着棒球棒对付托尼是否超过了必要限度？

艾莉：您知道当时托尼很凶，根本没有办法让他停下来。不过，棒球棒确实让他害怕了！

爸爸：明白了，看来用棒球棒对付托尼也是合理的，毕竟你们俩根本不是他的对手。那瑞安是不是可以下手轻点呢？

艾莉：您没在场，当时情势很紧张，我都吓坏了。在那种情况下，要求瑞安精确地把握轻重是很难的。我估计，瑞安当时想的就是让托尼不能还手，让他不能逃跑去拿刀。

爸爸：确实，不能事后用冷静的心态去衡量瑞安当时应该打到什么程度，用多少力量。事实上，许多不法侵害都是突然发生的，防卫者在紧张状态下，往往难以准确地判断侵害行为的程度，因此也很难周全地选择防卫手段。

艾莉：我同意防卫过当应该承担法律责任。但是，正当防卫的实质是以正义的行为对抗不法的行为，所以，法律应该优先保护防卫者,这样才能树立良好的社会示范。

爸爸:同意!你知道"校园霸凌"这个词吗?

艾莉:当然知道。

爸爸:你怎么看?

艾莉:我们学校对此零容忍,我很赞同。

爸爸:有些家长认为这只是小孩子之间的事情,不必那么认真。

艾莉:我是学生,我最有发言权。如果一个学生在学校遇到以大欺小、以强欺弱的情况,不仅他的身体可能受到伤害,而且最致命的是,他可能始终处于恐惧之中,不知道什么时候还会被欺负。

爸爸:看来,这会对孩子的生理和心理造成伤害。

艾莉:而且,如果不及时制止,其他同学看到了可能也会效仿,您想这些被欺负的同学在学校怎么待下去!

爸爸:如果你遇到这样的情况,要第一时间告诉爸爸妈妈和老师,我们会坚决制止,不能让学校霸凌有任何生存的土壤!

艾莉:前两天我看到了一个案例,佛罗里达州一个14岁的男生,在校车上被几个高年级的同学集体欺负,他拿刀反抗,刺伤了几个同学,后来法官判他无罪,法律就应该这样!

爸爸:我想这次托尼应该吸取教训了。

艾莉:这下我就放心了!

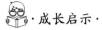·成长启示·

在学校或者日常生活中,如果遇到不法分子正在实施侵害自己或者他人的不法行为,防卫者采取必要的制止行为导致施害人受到伤害的,防卫者的行为是正当防卫行为,其无须承担法律责任。但是,正当防卫行为不能超过必要的限度,否则便构成防卫过当,对由此造成的损害后果,防卫者要承担一定的法律责任。

校园霸凌行为可能给孩子的身体和心理造成极大的伤害,危害严重。如果孩子在学校或者日常生活中遇到这种情况,要及时告知学校和家长,学校和家长会采取措施,坚决制止这种不法行为,法律会让校园霸凌行为受到惩罚。

·成长思考·

1. 瑞安为什么拿着棒球棒追打托尼?
2. 你如何看待学校霸凌行为?
3. 如果你是瑞安你会怎么办?

Chapter 9

Right to Self Defense

🕮 Reading Guide

Ellie and Ryan were both members of the school fencing team. Every day, the two went home together after practice. On their way home, they encountered Tony. Tony started to bully Ryan, which resulted in Ryan fighting back. Moreover, Ryan took a baseball bat and ran after Tony. What happened? If Tony was injured, should Ryan bear legal responsibility?

Ryan was a new student at Ellie's school. He was skinny with curly hair and black eyes that were full of life. Ryan also loved to fence: he started fencing when he was 6 years old and had become quite accomplished. He tried out for the fencing team at school and not only made the team and became the best fencer on the school fencing team just a few days after the season kicked off but also attracted a group of "fans".

While Ellie loved volleyball and played on a club team, the school did not have a volleyball team, prompting her to join the school fencing team and started fencing foil. While Ellie was a beginner, she picked up on fencing very quickly due to her talent in sports. Ryan also fenced foil and frequently gave Ellie advice to help Ellie with her posture and her steps.

One day after school, Ellie and her teammates went to the athletic center; everyone was talking and laughing amongst each other as they prepared for warm-ups. Ryan was the last one to step into the gym, and he threw his bags on the ground and did not greet anyone. When the team started to practice on the strips, Ryan did not pay attention and lost many rounds to his opponents. He even lost to people who he had never lost to before! What happened? Ellie could not help but wonder.

At the end of practice, everyone said goodbye and left the athletic center, leaving only Ellie and Ryan there.

"Ryan, your mind seems to be elsewhere today. What's going on?" Ellie asked caringly.

"Well ... nothing." Ryan lowered his head. His tone carried a tint of hesitation.

"If you need any help, you can tell me, and maybe I can help, " Ellie proposed enthusiastically.

After hesitating, Ryan finally asked, "It is Tony. Are you familiar with him?"

"I know him! He is a notorious bully from our neighboring

school. He used to bully other students, resulting in two warnings from his school. I've heard that he's gotten a bit better in 11th grade. Why did you ask? Did he bully you?" Ellie asked.

"I wouldn't say that. On the way to athletic center today, I met him when I passed by the parking lot. He yelled at me from the car. He threatened me to stay away from his car and said that I must obey what he says. Otherwise, he said that he would show me what he is capable of next time. He also warned me to be careful of his knife." Although Ryan looked calm, Ellie could still feel the frustration and dismay in his voice.

"Did he really do that? Do you want to talk to a teacher or to the principal so that the adults could report this situation to his school?" Ellie proposed angrily.

"I don't think that is necessary for now. Maybe he was just joking. Besides, I am a new student. If I am known as the 'tattletale who tells the teacher everything,' it would not turn out well for me. I can handle it myself," Ryan responded, lifting his head with a bit more confidence.

"Well, then take care of yourself. Maybe it's really nothing," Ellie encouraged.

Over the next few days of training, Ryan regained his confidence and rediscovered his passion for fencing, and he continued to be invincible. At the end of Thursday's practice,

Ryan was in a particularly good mood because he won every round that day. Ellie's performance that day was also quite impressive: she had won four out of five rounds!

"A few days ago, you helped me correct my move for retreating. It turned out to be very effective. I feel that my retreats were on point today," Ellie seized the opportunity to express her gratitude to Ryan.

"Those are my personal tricks. I would not teach them to anyone else!" Ryan said, smiling warmly.

"Of course! I am not going to teach the tricks to anyone else," Ellie joked. "In order to express my appreciation, the Mango Dragon Fruit Refresher from Starbucks is on me today," she added.

"Sounds good! I am extra thirsty today!" Ryan replied.

Ellie and Ryan carried their bags and walked through the parking lot to Starbucks. Ellie noticed that Ryan's backpack seemed heavier than the one he carried a couple of days ago. Before Ellie could ask what was in his bag, she saw a tall and familiar figure coming toward them from afar.

"It's Tony! What an unfortunate coincidence!" Ellie thought to herself.

Tony seemed to have recognized Ryan, so he walked straight to them.

"Little guy, why do I run into you all the time!" Tony started cursing as he tried to shove Ryan. However, Ryan quickly moved to the side, causing Tony to trip.

Ryan's move seemed to have irritated Tony, and he tried to hit Ryan again. This time, Ryan did not react fast enough to avoid the punch, which landed heavily on Ryan's left shoulder, causing him to stumble backwards. Tony raised his fist, intending to punch Ryan again, but Ryan took a step back, avoided Tony's punch and then threw a straight punch hitting the left side of Tony's face. Tony was stunned and did not see that Ryan was preparing to punch him again — that punch landed heavily on the right side of Tony's face.

Before Tony could react, Ryan turned to run, yelling and shouting as he went, "Ellie, hurry! Run home!"

Tony had never been subjected to such an attack before — he was always the one who landed a punch. He chased after Ryan like a mad lion, and because he was taller and stronger, he caught up with Ryan in a few steps. Tony grabbed Ryan's neck from behind and threw him onto the ground.

"Tony, stop! Stop hitting him, or else I will call the police!" Ellie shrieked.

Tony suddenly let go of Ryan and started to run away. Ellie realized that Ryan had pulled a baseball bat from his bag (that's why his bag looked heavier than usual!) and was running after Tony. Tony stumbled over a rock and slowed down, which allowed for Ryan to catch up to him. Ryan lifted the bat and swung at Tony. Tony fell to the ground, unconscious with blood flowing down along the side of his face. Ellie was shocked by this sudden scene; her jaw dropped, and she did not and could not make a sound. Ryan seemed stunned by what he had done as well. The bat fell from his hand to the ground. Eventually, Ellie came back to reality, quickly took out her phone, and called the police and the ambulance while Ryan took a towel from his bag and compressed Tony's wound with it. After a while, the police and the ambulance arrived. The medical staff quickly carried Tony to the ambulance, and they headed straight to the hospital.

The policeman asked, "What is going on?"

"It's me. I was the one who caused all the damage," Ryan's voice was trembling.

"What about you?" the police asked Ellie.

"I am his classmate. We were heading home from school," Ellie whispered.

"If that is the case, Ryan, I need you to come to the police station for further investigation. It is quite late now, so I need Ellie to leave her phone number. If necessary, we will contact you and your parents," the police said.

After seeing Ryan get on the police car, Ellie ran all the way back home. With Mom and Dad both present, Ellie told them about what happened just now.

Seeing Ellie's body tremble, Mom wrapped her arms around Ellie. "It's okay, Ellie. It's okay. It will be all right!"

When she arrived at the school the next day, Ellie was called to the principal's office. The police were also in the principal's office.

After Ellie retold the story in detail, the police asked, "Did Ryan ever mention that he had a baseball bat in his backpack?"

Ellie took a few moments to recall, but she eventually said, "No, he didn't tell me. A few days ago, he told me that Tony threatened him, and I told him to be careful."

"When Ryan swung at Tony with a bat, did Tony attack Ryan back?" the police continued.

Ellie was silent for a while, but she answered, "At the time, Tony was running away from Ryan. It looked as if he slipped and almost fell, so he did not attack Ryan."

"Did Ryan tell you why he was chasing and attacking Tony?" the police asked.

"I was so frightened to see that Tony was lying in a pool of blood. I asked Ryan why he swung at Tony with so much force. Ryan said that Tony was planning to retrieve his knife from the car, so ..." Ellie muttered.

"OK, I have no further questions. Please go to class," the police said.

"How is Ryan?" Ellie asked eagerly as the police were getting ready to leave.

"Ryan will continue to cooperate with the ongoing investigation this morning and will come back to school in the afternoon," the police finished and got up to depart from the principal's office.

Ellie was in a bad mood for the remainder of the day.

At dinner, Dad told Ellie that he had just called the principal, and the principal said that Tony had been diagnosed with a moderate concussion, which meant that he needed to be hospitalized, but it would not be life-threatening. Ellie couldn't help but discuss this with her father.

Ellie: Dad, do you think Ryan's actions counted as self-defense?

Dad: Wow, you are cutting straight into this problem!

Ellie: I did my research online!

Dad: Based on your research, what did you learn?

Ellie: On the Internet, self-defense is defined as the actions of those who are defending themselves against illegal infringements upon their rights. If such actions do not cause severe consequences, the actions count as self-defensive actions, and the defender would not have to bear legal responsibility. In other words, if Ryan's behavior is considered as legitimate self-defense, then Ryan would not have to bear legal responsibility.

Dad: Let's first take a look at the cause of the incident.

Ellie: On our way home following practice, Tony stopped us and started to harass and attack Ryan.

Dad: Who started the fight?

Ellie: Tony did, obviously! He first pushed Ryan and later punched him.

Dad: It seems that Tony was at fault.

Ellie: He had threatened Ryan before.

Dad: What kind of behavior was Tony's behavior?

Ellie: It obviously was unacceptable and wrong behavior!

Dad: No one had the right to infringe on the body integrity of others, unless it is for statutory reasons such as official duties. Tony's behavior was an act of illegally violating another person's body. His actions impaired and threatened the health and safety of Ryan.

Ellie: Official duties? Statutory reasons? Can you give an example?

Dad: One example would be the police chasing a fugitive

and ending up firing a gun.

Ellie: In the incident of rescuing a drowning person — like when Leo punched Owen so that he would stop struggling against him — would this also be considered a statutory reason?

Dad: Yes, that was done in an urgent situation to avoid harm or loss of life. This is an example of a statutory event. In the case of a statutory event, even if an action causes damage to others, there is no legal liability for the perpetrator.

Ellie: Ha-ha! That is a big thumb-up for me!

Dad: Right to self-defense requires the illegal acts to be objective, and it cannot be imagined.

Ellie: Is there such a thing as an imaginary violation?

Dad: For example, you mentioned that Tony had threatened Ryan before. If Tony didn't plan on beating Ryan when they ran into each other, but Ryan mistakenly thought that Tony would hurt him, that would be an example of an imaginary violation. In fact, the damage did not exist.

Ellie: Understood. In that case, if Ryan hit Tony, it would not be a legitimate act of self-defense.

Dad: Did Ryan fight back?

Ellie: Yes, after Tony hit Ryan, Ryan fought back.

Dad: Ryan's counterattack was used to stop Tony's illegal infringement. It was an act to protect himself from harm. This was a kind of self-defense.

Ellie: Therefore, Ryan's actions were justified and protected by the law, right? If a person is beaten, there is no way that the law forbids the defender to fight back, right?

Dad: Of course, protecting your own safety is the most basic right of all.

Ellie: I agree with that. When coming in contact with illegal infringements, the law must not only encourage people to fight back actively but also encourage bystanders to help others in need.

Dad: Self-defense is justified when an illegal offense is taking place. If the infringement has not yet occurred or is already over, then the defender's actions will not be justified by and classified as their right to self-defense.

Ellie: Can you give an example?

Dad: For example, suppose Tony didn't continue to beat Ryan up after Ryan's punch and they went home and went on with their evening. Afterward, if Ryan became more and more frustrated and found Tony again to beat Tony up with his baseball bat, then it would not be an example of a justified act of self-defense because the infringement had already been over.

Ellie: That would be considered as revenge.

Dad: Do you think the law should encourage or protect

such actions of revenge?

Ellie: No. After all, revenge will only cause new damage.

Dad: Yes, and the law does not encourage counterviolence!

Ellie: However, the feeling of being bullied is not pleasant, and sometimes it is hard to eliminate the anger.

Dad: Don't worry. The law will punish those who bully others.

Ellie: So, in this situation, Ryan's actions were carried out during an infringement of his personal rights, correct?

Dad: At the time, Tony was chasing after Ryan. Then, why did Tony suddenly run away?

Ellie: Ryan took out the baseball bat from his backpack. Tony got scared, so he turned and fled.

Dad: Is it possible to think that Tony's infringement upon Ryan's rights had ended by then?

Ellie: Hey, it seems like I have fallen into your trap!

Dad: I didn't mean for that to happen!

Ellie: However, we were all scared at the time, and we didn't know if Tony would hurt Ryan again. Ryan later said that he thought that Tony escaped in order to grab the knife from his car.

Dad: In other words, it was difficult for Ryan to determine accurately whether or not the infringement had ended?

Ellie: It was not just difficult; it was impossible! We did not know what Tony was planning on doing. Perhaps he was really getting his knife. Did you know that Tony used to bully classmates and that we were all afraid of him?

Dad: It seems that there was a continued possibility of Tony hurting other people.

Ellie: It seems that you really didn't purposely try to trick me. Thank you for that!

Dad: Do you think Ryan's swing was a bit too strong?

Ellie: Here comes the trap again! I know that you want to ask whether or not Ryan's defensive behavior was over the top.

Dad: Yes, even if one's behavior is a legitimate act of self-defense, if it exceeds the necessary limits, it will constitute an excessive defense, and it could mean that the defender would need to bear a certain amount of legal responsibility.

Ellie: This is a high standard to meet!

Dad: Think about it: why are these standards even there?

Ellie: Even though the purpose of self-defense is to protect the victim from further harm, it can result in excessive damage to the perpetrator.

Dad: Yes. Although legitimate acts of self-defense help prevent the wrongful acts of the perpetrators, they sometimes cause some harm to the perpetrators. Therefore, it has some elements of counterviolence. If there is no limit on the extent of defense, it is unfair to the perpetrators to allow the victims to act however they want to.

Ellie: So, how do you judge whether or not a defensive act exceeds the necessary limits?

Dad: This is a little bit complicated, and it must be considered according to the specific situations.

Ellie: Is there any standardized rule?

Dad: Under normal circumstances, if the defensive behavior clearly exceeds the necessary limits and causes serious consequences, it would be classified as an excessive defense. That is to say, in some cases, in order to stop certain wrongdoings, it is evident that some extreme measures are not necessary. If one takes excessive actions, the defender is considered to "have exceeded the necessary limits."

Ellie: Is it kind of like killing a fly with a spear?

Dad: Something like that. For example, if someone slaps you across the face, you don't have to use a machete to defend yourself.

Ellie: I understand now. A slap across the face will only cause physical pain, while the machete might cause death! This is a glaring example of excessive self-defense.

Dad: So, in order to stop Tony from hurting him, did

Ryan's action of holding a baseball bat as an act of self-defense exceed the necessary limits?

Ellie: I want you to know that Tony was very fierce at the time, and there was no way to stop him. However, the baseball bat really did scare him!

Dad: I understand. It seemed reasonable to use a baseball bat to scare Tony. After all, the two of you were definitely not as strong as he is. However, was it possible for Ryan to swing a little bit lighter?

Ellie: You were not present. The situation was very nerve-wracking, and I was scared. In that case, it was challenging to demand Ryan to control the amount of force applied precisely. I am guessing that what Ryan wanted at the time was to prevent Tony from fighting back so that Tony could not go to his car to retrieve the knife.

Dad: Indeed, we can't measure the extent to which Ryan could have moderated his swing because he was panicked at the time. In fact, many unlawful infringements occur out of the blue. It is often difficult for victims to accurately determine the extent of force necessary to stop the perpetrator. Therefore, it is difficult to choose carefully the means of defense in an urgent situation.

Ellie: I agree that someone who excessively defends himself or herself should bear legal responsibilities for the actions.

However, the essence of legitimate self-defense is to act justly against unlawful behaviors. Therefore, the law should prioritize the protection of victims. Only then can the law establish a superb social demonstration.

Dad: Yes! Have you heard of the term "school bullying"?

Ellie: I have, of course.

Dad: What do you think about it?

Ellie: Our school has zero-tolerance for school bullying, and I agree with the policy.

Dad: Some parents think that this is just joking around between children, and it is nothing serious.

Ellie: I am a student, so I have the right to comment on this. If a student encounters bullying at school, not only can his physical body get hurt, but he may also be constantly living in the fear of being bullied again.

Dad: So, bullying hurts a child physically and emotionally.

Ellie: And, if you don't stop it in time, other students might start bullying the victim. If that happens, there is no way that the bullied ones can get through school days!

Dad: If you encounter such a situation, you must tell your parents and the teachers immediately. We will step in because we cannot let school bullying spread and prosper!

Ellie: I saw a case on the news a couple of days ago. A 14-year-old boy from Florida was bullied by several upperclassmen on the school bus. In resistance, he grabbed a knife and stabbed several of the bullies. While it is very sad that the situation escalated to that kind of violence, I was happy to learn that a judge determined that the boy was not guilty because he had been bullied so badly. This is the way that laws should be!

Dad: I think that this time, Tony should be able to learn from his mistake.

Ellie: I feel so much more relieved now!

 Growth Revelation

In school or in life, if a perpetrator is carrying out a wrongful act against a person or a third party, the person can take the necessary measures to prevent harm. If the measures cause the perpetrator to be harmed, the actions will be considered to be legitimate measures of self-defense, and the defender does not need to bear legal responsibilities for the actions. However, lawful defensive behavior cannot exceed the necessary limits; otherwise, it will constitute an excessive defense, and the defender must bear specific legal responsibilities for the damage caused.

School bullying may cause significant harm to children's physical and mental health, and the consequences are severe. If a child encounters such a situation in or outside of school, the school and the parents should be informed in a timely manner. The school and the parents should take measures to stop the illegal behavior immediately, and the law will punish the bully for his or her actions.

Think and Consider

1. Why did Ryan chase after Tony with a baseball bat?
2. What is your view on school bullying?
3. If you were in Ryan's situation, what would you do?

第十章
我的作品我做主

·导读·

艾莉为了完成主题为"恐惧"的绘画,苦思冥想,费尽心思。最后,她从一个古老的中国爱情故事中获得了灵感。当艾莉怀着忐忑的心情把作品呈现给老师时,老师沉默了。你觉得老师和同学们会喜欢她的作品吗?学生的绘画作品学校可以擅自使用吗?

艾莉喜欢画画,每次看到五颜六色的颜料,就禁不住想画上几笔。不忙的时候,她每天放学回家都会画一会儿。不过,艾莉不喜欢画素描,因为她觉得素描色彩太简单了,用艾莉自己的话说,素描"单调、枯燥、无聊"。尽管艾莉知道素描是绘画的基础,也明白"基础不牢,画画不好"的道理,但是一直对素描兴趣不大。

暑假里,妈妈"强迫"艾莉报了素描班,艾莉一口气画了40多幅素描作品。慢慢地,艾莉发现,素描虽然只有黑白两种颜色,但是同样能表现出很多层次。尤其是看到自己素描画出的苹果好像要从纸上掉下来的时候,艾莉似乎真正感受到了光和影的魅力。

妈妈说艾莉画画有点开窍了，艾莉自己也觉得，一个暑假"枯燥"的训练大大提高了自己的素描水平，现在她画画时对轮廓把握得更准确了，也就是妈妈常常要求的"画什么像什么"。看来还是应了那句老话：最简单的往往是最重要的。

去年参加夏令营时，艾莉创作了一幅作品《融合》。没想到，这幅作品被一家礼品公司看中了。礼品公司征得艾莉同意后，用她的设计作品做出了杯垫、布包等小礼品，当看到这些小礼品时，艾莉简直不敢相信自己的眼睛。礼品公司还告诉她，上线第一天，杯垫就卖了50多套，生意不错。自己的设计居然变成了商品，还能赚到钱，这大大超出了艾莉的想象，以至于很长一段时间里，艾莉都不敢相信这是真的。

这学期艾莉选修了创意绘画课。老师给出题目，同学们根据自己的想法创作，作品类型不限，这给了艾莉很大的想象空间，她已经完成的几幅作品老师都很满意。周三上课时，老师说本期绘画主题为"恐惧"，要求大家在两周之内完成。这下可难住了艾莉，因为艾莉觉得描写恐惧的东西很多，很难创新，另外自己也没什么恐惧的。艾莉毫无头绪，下课时画板上一片空白，草稿纸倒是用了不少。一连几天，艾莉满脑子都在想着"恐惧"，见到熟悉的同学就问："你恐惧什么？"同学们都说她走火入魔了。

周五放学回家，妈妈正在做晚饭，艾莉见到妈妈便问：

"妈妈，你恐惧什么？"

妈妈被艾莉的突然发问弄得"丈二和尚摸不着头脑"，张着嘴巴，一时不知道说什么好。

"看到你这样子，我就很恐惧。"艾莉被妈妈机智的回答逗笑了，妈妈也笑了。

晚上，艾莉一家人坐在一起看电影，电影讲的是一个古老的中国故事。一个贵族公子赶庙会，遇到了一个女子，女子戴着美丽的面具。公子一时好奇就摘下了女子的面具，发现女子竟是当朝公主。公主一下子爱上了英俊的公子，公子也爱上了公主。国王命令公子迎娶公主，可是公子已经成婚，于是国王下令，赐死了公子的妻子。公子万分内疚，在和公主完婚之夜，吞剑自尽。

看着看着，艾莉突然起身往楼上跑，边跑边说："妈妈、妈妈！我想到了，我去网上查资料！"

妈妈缓过神，忙问："你想到什么了？你慢点，小心楼梯！"

艾莉没有回答，不过，爸爸妈妈似乎猜到了什么，相视一笑。

接下来一周，艾莉做完作业就把自己关在房间里，上网查资料、打底、动笔……全家人都知道她在忙什么，所以也不去打扰她。

周三上课，艾莉怀着忐忑的心情把自己的作品递给了老师。老师看着作品，沉默了足足一分钟多的时间，这一分钟对艾莉来说好似一年。老师抬起头，严肃地看着艾莉，突然又笑了，对她说："你居然画了一副面具，而且是如此美丽的一副面具，从轮廓到色彩都很美丽，但是我在美丽之下似乎感受到了极大的恐惧！"

一句话说得艾莉险些掉下眼泪，她语无伦次地向老师讲述自己的创作灵感，讲那个凄美的东方爱情故事，还告诉老师，她为此连续看了两遍《剧院魅影》。老师也很激动，说："我马上把这幅作品推荐到学校画廊展出。"

学校画廊是展示全校学生优秀绘画作品的地方，是每个学生心中的艺术殿堂，能在这里展出自己的作品是莫大的荣誉。一连几天，艾莉都有事没事地往画廊那边逛，远远地看着同学们围在自己的作品前指指点点，心中美滋滋的。

转眼又到了学校一年一度的义卖节。艾莉很喜欢参加学校的义卖节，因为在义卖节上，她不仅可以把自己不用的东西卖掉，而且还能淘到不少自己喜欢的便宜货。不过很遗憾，今年的义卖节刚好和击剑队的校际对抗赛冲突，艾莉要参加对抗赛，所以只能遗憾地错过了。

义卖节第二天一大早，艾莉刚到学校就迫不及待地问费利西娅："昨天义卖节哪件物品最受欢迎呀？"

"啊？你不知道吗？是我们学校的新年挂历呀，上面有你的作品《面具》。估计不少人是冲着你的这幅作品买挂历的，我买了好几本，准备送给朋友。"费利西娅也不忘抓住机会夸赞自己的朋友。

"挂历？有我的作品？我怎么不知道？"艾莉迟疑了一下。

看到艾莉将信将疑，费利西娅连忙从书包里拿出一本挂历，递给了艾莉。

的确是新年挂历，非常精美，而且第一幅就是自己创作的《面具》。不知怎么，艾莉一点都高兴不起来，心情有些复杂！回到家，艾莉和爸爸聊起了这件事。

艾莉：爸爸，您觉得《面具》是不是我的财产？

爸爸：在回答你的问题之前，我们先讨论一下什么是财产，可以吗？

艾莉：这个问题听起来简单，回答起来还有点困难！

爸爸：那你可以举几个财产的例子吗？

艾莉：这个简单！屋子里的桌子、椅子、电视机，书桌上的笔和本子，我手里的手机，这些都是财产。

爸爸：当然，房子也是我们家的财产。

艾莉：对，忘了，这是我们家重要的财产！

爸爸：这些物品有什么共性吗？

艾莉：都需要用钱买，只是有的贵，有的便宜罢了。

爸爸：对，它们都可以用金钱衡量。

艾莉：另外，这些财产各有各的用途。

爸爸：很好！财产都有它的使用价值。

艾莉：其他的我暂时还没想出来。

爸爸：空气有使用价值吗？

艾莉：当然，离开空气谁也活不了。

爸爸：阳光呢？

艾莉：生物学上讲，阳光是生命存在的必要条件之一。

爸爸：但是，法律上一般不把这些列为财产。想想看，为什么？

艾莉：它们不能用金钱衡量？可是网上说，有人用罐子装了北极的空气回来卖。

爸爸：我也看到了这则新闻，感觉有点"博眼球"的味道。

艾莉：不过，如果太阳、空气成了个人财产，我们的生活可能会很恐怖。

爸爸：我们每天起床后要买新鲜空气！

艾莉：哈哈，每天买阳光？有点不可思议！

爸爸：空气、阳光这些东西都有一个共同的特点：它们都是我们人类个体无法控制的。

艾莉：因为无法控制，所以很难区分出它们是谁的。

爸爸：因此，即使它们有使用价值，法律上通常也不会把它们界定为财产。

艾莉：明白！

爸爸：所以法律意义上的财产是人类能够控制的，有使用价值，并且能够用金钱衡量的。

艾莉：放眼望去，我们屋里屋外都是财产。

爸爸：这些财产都是看得见、摸得着的。

艾莉：还有看不见、摸不着的财产？

爸爸：有！

艾莉：我知道了，您说的是类似发明创造这样的财产吧？以前我们计算机课的老师讲过。

爸爸：这些财产的价值主要体现在它们的思想或者内容上，体现出的是人的智力成果，通常没有一定的形状，所以也叫知识资产或者无形资产。

艾莉：明白了。

爸爸：你能再举些无形财产的例子吗？

艾莉：书籍！

爸爸：书籍是智者，是人类永恒的老师。

艾莉：同样是书籍，差别也很大，有的是不朽名著，有的是"快消品"。

爸爸：《战争与和平》《了不起的盖茨比》这样的名著价值连城！

艾莉：软件程序！

爸爸：一个应用软件可能开创一个企业王国。

艾莉：音乐，还有绘画作品！

爸爸：快要回到正题了。当然，知识财产还有很多！

艾莉：我记得，老师告诉我们，做作业引用网上图片时，一定要引用已公开而且可以使用的图片，引用其他文章的内容一定要写明出处，否则会侵犯别人的知识产权。

爸爸：给你们老师点个赞！

艾莉：网上有很多好看的图片，原本我还真以为用用也没关系呢。

爸爸：法律规定知识产权受法律保护，未经许可，任何人不可以仿冒或擅自使用他人的专利、音乐或绘画作品等知识资产，否则要承担赔偿责任，严重的还要承担刑事责任。

艾莉：同意！

爸爸：一项发明创造的出炉常常要花费几年的时间，甚至耗费科学家毕生的精力。

艾莉：这个我特别能理解，创作《面具》时，我花了很多的时间和精力进行构思和创新。

爸爸：有些发明创造还要付出很大的代价或成本。

艾莉：我以前看到过一个报告，它说一款新药的研发可能要花费几亿甚至十几亿美元，而且还经常失败。

爸爸：有些知识产权的商业价值巨大！你不是喜欢喝可口可乐嘛。

艾莉：现在喝得少了。

爸爸：据说可口可乐的配方被锁在一个秘密的保险柜里。

艾莉：如果配方泄露了，后果不堪设想！

爸爸：一部手机可能涉及上千个专利，如果不保护这些专利，手机厂商辛辛苦苦研发的新手机很快就会被别人仿冒，这不但会导致手机厂商巨大的经济损失，而且还会影响科学家进行创造的积极性。

艾莉：所以，法律要严格保护知识产权，保护社会公平，保护创造者的积极性。

爸爸：只有这样，科技才能不断地进步，不断地改变我们的生活！

艾莉：完全同意！

爸爸：手机是你的财产，你对它有什么具体的权利呢？

艾莉：我可以用它打电话、玩游戏。

爸爸：你的手机，你有使用权。不过，玩游戏还是要有节制。

艾莉：我可以把我的手机送给妈妈。

爸爸：嗯，你妈妈听了一定会很高兴。所有权人可以自由处分自己的财产，如转让、赠送，甚至销毁，等等。当然，你是未成年人，你处分贵重物品时必须事先征得我和你妈妈的同意。

艾莉：我明白，你们是我的监护人。

爸爸：还有呢？

艾莉：我可以把手机带在身上，不让别人碰。

爸爸：法律上这叫占有，所有权人对自己的财产享有占有的权利。

艾莉：上次听妈妈说，暑假我们外出旅行时，可能会把我们家的房子短期租给彼得叔叔，因为他的朋友要来旅游。

爸爸：这事儿还没确定。

艾莉： 租出去吧，这样我们就可以收一大笔租金了！

爸爸： 这是收益权。总结起来，一项财产的所有人对自己的财产至少拥有四项基本权益：占有它、使用它、处分它以及处分后获得收益的权利。

艾莉： 如果我们把房子租出去了，房子还是我们的吧？

爸爸： 那是当然。房子出租了，所有权还是我们的，但是使用权属于彼得叔叔了。所以，财产所有权的四项基本权益可以全部由一个人享有，也可以由不同的人分别使用和享有。

艾莉： 明白了！

爸爸： 那我们回到正题。现在我们已经明确绘画作品是一项知识产权，应该受法律保护，那么，《面具》应该归谁所有呢？

艾莉： 我觉得应该归我所有。想想看，《面具》的创意是我的，又是我画的，为了这幅画我付出了很多时间和精力，所以，它应该归我所有。

爸爸： 如果归你所有，那你对《面具》可以享有什么权利呢？

艾莉： 按照刚才的讨论：我可以把它挂在家里，也可以经学校同意把它挂在画廊展出；我可以自己留着，也可以把它卖掉。总之，如果《面具》归我所有，未经我的同意，学校不可以擅自使用它或者把它印制成挂历，也不可以销售。

爸爸： 事实上，法律规定知识产权原则上应归创造者所有，以此保护创造者的利益和创新积极性，维护社会公平。

艾莉：太好了！不过，我有个问题。

爸爸：说说看。

艾莉：您刚才提到手机厂商有成千上万个专利，我知道很多软件都是由工程师开发的，那么这些知识产权是归工程师个人所有呢，还是归公司所有？

爸爸：很好的问题！想想看，这些工程师和你有什么不同？

艾莉：他们开发软件是完成工作任务。

爸爸：这是两者最大的区别。工程师们开发软件是其本职工作，公司为此支付了他们工资，所以，他们的工作成果应该归公司所有。即使这样，在软件的著作权中也要列示开发者的个人名字，这叫署名权。

艾莉：我明白了。我画这幅画虽然是在完成学校的作业，但是学校没有付我报酬，所以作品应该归我所有。如果学校想要使用我的作品，应该征得我的同意。事实上，我也不是反对学校使用我的作品印制挂历，但是他们至少应该征求一下我的意见，或者听听我的建议吧。

爸爸：有些学校，尤其是一些艺术学校，在入学时都会和学生签署协议，约定他们的绘画作品学校可以在一定的范围内使用，如参加巡展、推荐参加比赛等。所以，我建议你去问问你妈妈，有没有和学校签过类似的合同。

艾莉：明白了，合同相当于我和学校之间的法律。我马上就去问问妈妈!

·成长启示·

专利、商标、绘画、书籍、音乐等都属于知识产权保护范围,受到法律保护。任何人未经许可,不得擅自使用他人的智力成果,否则要承担法律责任。

学生在学校的绘画作品是由学生创造的,它不同于公司员工的职务作品,因此,其著作权原则上属于学生所有。除非学校和学生之间有特殊约定,否则学校也不能随意使用学生的作品。

·成长思考·

1. 为了完成作品《面具》,艾莉做了哪些努力?
2. 你觉得什么是财产?
3. 你觉得法律为什么应该保护知识财产?

Chapter 10

I'm in Charge of My Work!

📖 Reading Guide

To complete the painting with the theme of "fear," Ellie thought intensely about what she could draw that would accomplish the task. Finally, she was inspired by an old Chinese love story. When Ellie presented her work to the teacher, the teacher fell silent. Do you think teachers and classmates would like her work? Can a student's work be used by the school without an authorization?

Ellie loved painting. Every time she saw a variety of colorful paints, Ellie felt compelled to use those paints to create beautiful paintings. When she was not busy with schoolwork, Ellie loved to come home and work on her art pieces. Sketching, on the other hand, was Ellie's least favorite artistic activity. In Ellie's words, sketching was "monotonous and boring." Although Ellie knew that sketching was a fundamental exercise — the basics of any realistic and even abstract art — she still couldn't get herself to be interested in sketching.

Over the summer, Ellie's mom convinced her to attend a sketching class during which she worked on more than forty pieces. Gradually, Ellie realized that even with only black and white, there were still so many different shades that could demonstrate the different textures and layers of an object. When she saw that the apple she drew was so realistic and looked as if it had been an actual apple, Ellie really felt the charm of lights and shadows.

Ellie's mom admired her sketching and said that her paintings were improving as well, and Ellie herself also felt that a summer's "boring" training had dramatically improved her artistic abilities. Now she could draw more accurate outlines, just as what her mother had always expected to see in her. Just as the old proverb says, the simplest is often the most important.

Last year, Ellie attended a summer camp and created a piece called "Fusion." Surprisingly, her work impressed a gift company. The company offered her a deal in which they used her artwork in their designs of coasters, handbags, and other related gifts. When Ellie saw these products, she blinked many times to make sure that she was not dreaming. The company also told her that on the first day, they sold more than fifty sets of products with her designs! Ellie was fascinated by the fact that her designs had become products and made her so much money. For a long time, Ellie couldn't believe it was true.

This past semester, she enrolled in Creative Drawing as her elective. In this course, the teacher would pick a theme each class, and the students would create a piece that they felt represented that theme. Because she had the choice of what media she wanted to use, Ellie could get as creative and expressive as she wanted to, allowing her to create several pieces that her teachers loved. On Wednesday, the teacher assigned "fear" as the theme of the week, giving the class two weeks to create their works. This was a challenge for Ellie because there were so many ways to represent such an abstract topic and because Ellie herself had nothing to be fearful of. By the end of class, she still hadn't drawn anything on her canvas, but she did have a pile of crumpled sketch paper! For the next few days, all Ellie could think about was "fear." Whenever she saw a friend in the hallway, she would ask, "How would you define fear?" The classmates all jokingly said that she was out of her mind.

When she got home on Friday, her mom was cooking dinner for the family. Ellie asked her mom, "Mom, what do you fear?"

Ellie's mom was truly confused by this sudden question completely lacking in context! She opened her mouth but was baffled.

"The way you look right now inflicts fear on me!" Ellie was amused by her mom's witty answer, and her mom broke into a smile.

In the evening, Ellie's family sat together to watch a movie about an old Chinese story. An aristocratic man was on his way to the temple fair when he met a woman who wore a beautiful mask. Curious to see who was behind the mask, he removed it and found that the woman was a princess. The princess and the young man fell in love with each other. The king ordered the man to marry the princess, but he was already married to someone. The king ordered that the man's wife be killed so that the man could marry the princess. The young man, however, felt very guilty for his wife's death, and on the night of the wedding with the princess, he took his own life by swallowing the sword.

Halfway through the movie, Ellie suddenly got up and rushed upstairs as she screamed, "Mom! I have an idea! I have to conduct some research!"

Mom gathered herself and asked hurriedly, "What is your idea? Slow down. Watch your steps!"

Ellie did not respond, but her parents seemed to know what was going on.

For the next week, whenever she had finished her

homework, Ellie focused exclusively on researching, sketching, and painting. Because everyone knew what she was working on, no one interrupted her working process.

The next Wednesday, Ellie handed in her project — nervous about how the teacher would react. The teacher looked at the work and was silent for what seemed like forever! Finally, the teacher looked up and smiled, "I didn't expect you to paint a mask, and especially not such a beautiful mask. It is beautiful from outline to the color, but I see the perfect representation of fear in this painting!"

This nearly made Ellie tear up, and she struggled to gather her words to explain to her teacher about her inspiration and the beautiful yet pitiful love story. She also told her teacher that she watched *Phantom of the Opera* twice for this piece of work. Her teacher was also beyond excited, "I am going to send this beautiful piece to the head of the art department and mount it for display in the school gallery!"

The school gallery was where the best of the best artworks were displayed, and it was an honor to have one's work shown there. For the next couple of days, Ellie frequently visited the art gallery. As she saw that many were enjoying her work, she could not hide her smile.

The semester progressed, and soon it was time to prepare

for the annual school sale. Ellie absolutely adored the yearly sale. Not only was this a great chance to promote her own works and products, but it was also a way for her to find products that she loved. Unfortunately, Ellie had a fencing meet on the day of the annual sale, so she would not have time to attend the sale this year.

The day after the big sale, Ellie rushed to talk to Felicia about the sale, "Tell me! Which product won the best-seller title this year?"

"Did you not hear about it? It's the school's newly designed calendar! Your painting, 'The Mask,' is featured on it. I'm betting that many people bought the calendar because of your work! I bought a couple because I think my friends will love them!" Felicia didn't forget to compliment Ellie for her great effort.

"School calendar? With my painting in it? Why wasn't I informed about it?" Ellie blinked.

Because Ellie looked confused, Felicia quickly pulled out a calendar from her bag and handed it to Ellie.

It definitely was a calendar for the upcoming year. The calendar was well-designed and packaged with care, and the first artwork featured was Ellie's work of "The Mask." However, Ellie was not able to cheer herself up at all. When she got home,

Ellie started a discussion with her dad.

Ellie: Dad, do you think my painting of "The Mask" is considered as my property?

Dad: Before answering your question, let's first talk about what property is. Is that OK with you?

Ellie: It sounds like an easy question. However, when you think about it, it is actually quite difficult to define!

Dad: Then, can you list some examples of property?

Ellie: That's easy! For instance, in a house, there are tables, chairs, televisions, the pens and notebooks on the desk, the phone in my hand, etc. These are all examples of property.

Dad: And, the house is also our property.

Ellie: Oh, right! I almost forgot! The house is an essential property of ours!

Dad: So, what do these items have in common?

Ellie: You can purchase all of these items with money.

Dad: Correct! Their values can be measured with money. However, some are more expensive than others.

Ellie: Also, all of these pieces of property have their own values and uses.

Dad: Yes! All property has its own use-value.

Ellie: That's all the characteristics of property I can think of for now.

Dad: Is air essential?

Ellie: Definitely! Without air, no one would survive.

Dad: How about sunlight?

Ellie: Biologically, sunlight is essential for life to be present on Earth.

Dad: Exactly. However, according to the law, these do not count as property. Think about it, why do you think that is?

Ellie: Is it because you cannot measure them with money? But I read a newspaper article saying that someone brought back fresh air from the North Pole using a jar and sold it for profit.

Dad: I saw that article as well. I feel like it was written purely for attention.

Ellie: However, if sunlight and air became personal property, our lives would change forever!

Dad: Maybe that would mean that we would have to purchase fresh air when we wake up every morning!

Ellie: Ha-ha! "Buying air every day"? That seems a little ridiculous!

Dad: Air and sunlight have something in common: they cannot be controlled or owned by a single individual.

Ellie: Because they cannot be manipulated, it is hard to distinguish or tell who these resources belong to.

Dad: Therefore, even though they are essential and valuable, the law would typically not classify them as property.

Ellie: Got it!

Dad: Therefore, according to the law, property has to be something that can be controlled or owned by individuals and useful to others. Additionally, its value has to be measurable using money or some type of currency.

Ellie: Looking at the definition now, property is all around us! Both in and outside our house!

Dad: All of these property is visible and tangible.

Ellie: Is there also invisible and intangible property?

Dad: Of course!

Ellie: Oh, I know what you are talking about! Are you talking about property like inventions? Our computer science teacher talked about that in class!

Dad: The value of such property is represented by the idea or information contained in it, usually in the form of human inventions or a representation of some type of human effort that is in no specific shape or form. Therefore, we classify them as intellectual or intangible assets.

Ellie: I understand now.

Dad: Can you name some more examples of intangible assets?

Ellie: Books are good examples!

Dad: Yes, books are like sages, who are eternal teachers of humanity.

Ellie: There are a lot of books, but all of them are different. Some are masterpieces created by masterminds, while others are just for laughs.

Dad: *War and Peace* and *The Great Gatsby* are both examples of immortal masterpieces that live on!

Ellie: Apps and programs are also personal property!

Dad: An app could be the start of an entire company.

Ellie: Music and artworks are also property!

Dad: We are getting closer to our original question. Of course, there are still plenty of examples of intellectual assets.

Ellie: I remember that our teacher told us that when we use pictures from online, we have to use the ones that are specifically labeled for reuse and cite the articles and resources used for our projects. Otherwise, it is considered plagiarism.

Dad: A big round of applause to your teacher!

Ellie: Before that, I saw many pretty pictures online. Initially, I thought it would be fine to use those pictures.

Dad: The law provides that intellectual property rights are protected by law. Without permission, no one can copy or arbitrarily use other people's intellectual property such as patents, music, or paintings. Those who do are liable for compensation or even criminal responsibility.

Ellie: I agree!

Dad: Creating an invention or product often takes a couple of years or even a scientist's lifetime.

Ellie: I can relate to what you just said. When I was painting "The Mask," it took an immense amount of effort to sketch and create.

Dad: Some inventions are also created at a high cost.

Ellie: I read a research paper once, and it said that the development of a new drug may cost hundreds of millions or even billions of dollars. It also takes many different trials to find an effective and safe treatment.

Dad: Exactly! Some intellectual property and patents carry an immense amount of commercial value! Don't you like to drink Coca-Cola?

Ellie: I used to, but not anymore.

Dad: Apparently, the recipe of Coca-Cola is locked up in a secret safe.

Ellie: If the recipe leaked, the result would result in the loss of a lot of money for the company! That could be catastrophic!

Dad: A phone might involve thousands of patents. If no one is there to protect these patents, the new phones that the manufacturers have worked so hard on will soon be copied by others. Not only will it cause a significant economic loss for the manufacturers, but it will also discourage scientists, causing them to lose the motivation to innovate new products.

Ellie: Therefore, the law needs to strictly protect intellectual property rights, the fairness of society, and the creators' enthusiasm for further innovations.

Dad: Only then can technology really improve continuously and change our lives in the future!

Ellie: I agree!

Dad: The phone is your property, so what rights do you have regarding the phone?

Ellie: I can use it to call other people or play games.

Dad: Your phone, your decision, but you should control how much you play.

Ellie: I can also give my phone to my mother as a gift.

Dad: Yes, and your mother would be very delighted to hear that. Owners have the right to do what they want with their property, such as selling it, giving it away as a gift, or even disposing of it. You, on the other hand, are a minor, so when you are handling your valuable belongings, your mother and I need to agree to it.

Ellie: I understand that. It is because you are my guardians.

Dad: What else?

Ellie: I can carry the phone with me and not allow anyone else to use it.

Dad: Legally, this is called possession, and owners have the right to possess their property.

Ellie: My mom told me that when we are on vacation during the summer, we might lend our house to Uncle Peter for a short period since his friends are coming over for a vacation.

Dad: We haven't entirely made up our minds yet.

Ellie: Let's rent it. We can make a lot of money merely from collecting rent!

Dad: This is the right to income. To sum up, owners of a property has at least four basic rights to the property: possession of it, usage of it, disposition of it, and the right to income after disposing of the property.

Ellie: If we put the house up for rent, it still belongs to us, correct?

Dad: Of course! If someone rents the house, we still have ownership of the house, but the right to use it for a specified period now belongs to someone else. Therefore, the four fundamental rights to a property can be possessed by a single individual or shared between many people.

Ellie: Ah! That makes sense!

Dad: Let's get back to the original question. Now that we have clearly stated that a piece of artwork is intellectual property and should be protected by law, who do you think your painting of "The Mask" belongs to?

Ellie: I think that it belongs to me. Considering that I came up with the idea and that I created the piece, I am the one that put the most amount of effort and time into this piece. Therefore, it should belong to me.

Dad: If it belongs to you, what rights do you have of this painting?

Ellie: According to the discussion that we just had, I can hang it at home or put it up for display in the school gallery. I can choose to keep it or sell it. In conclusion, if the painting belongs to me, the school can neither use it nor print it into calendars for profit without my permission.

Dad: In fact, the law stipulates that intellectual property rights should be owned by the creators to protect the interests of creators, to stimulate the enthusiasm for innovation, and to maintain social equity.

Ellie: That's amazing! I just have one more question.

Dad: Go ahead.

Ellie: You mentioned that phone manufacturers have thousands and millions of patents. I know that many programs are made by programmers in the company. So, do these programs technically belong to the developers themselves or the company?

Dad: That is a great question, but what are the differences between those computer engineers and you?

Ellie: Their job is to write and create programs.

Dad: This is a major difference. The engineers make new programs because it is part of their job. The company paid them to do so; therefore, their work should belong to the company. Even so, the developers' personal names should be listed in the copyright of the software. This is called the authorship.

Ellie: I get it now. Even though I finished the painting at school, the school did not pay me, so the piece should still belong to me. If the school wants to use my work, they should ask for my consent. In fact, I am not against the school using my work on the calendars, but they should have at least asked for my opinion or listened to my advice.

Dad: Some schools, especially some art schools, require you to sign a contract with them when you first arrive. The contract includes information about the usage of your work, such as display in the art galleries and attending contests. Therefore, I suggest that you should go talk to your mother about whether or not you have signed a similar contract.

Ellie: Understood! That contract is like a law between the school and me. I will go ask my mom now!

Growth Revelation

Patents, trademarks, paintings, books, music, etc. are all intellectual property and are protected by law. No one may use the intellectual property of another without permission; otherwise, they shall bear legal responsibility.

A student's painting at school is created by the student. It is different from works of a company's employees. Therefore, its copyright is typically owned by the student, unless there is a special agreement between the school and the student. Without such a special agreement, the school is not allowed to use the students' paintings without permission.

Think and Consider

1. To finish "The Mask," what kind of effort did Ellie put in?

2. What do you think is the definition of property?

3. Why do you think the law should protect intellectual property?

人们常常对法律心怀恐惧，不知道它背后隐藏着怎样的"秘密"，但是法律存在的意义正是消除人们对未知的恐惧，保护社会的稳定。正是因为有了法律的存在，我们才有了今日的文明和繁荣。

奥地利著名法学家欧根·埃利希曾经说过："法发展的重心不在立法，不在法学，也不在司法判决，而在社会本身。"随着时代的发展和科技的进步，人们对于"对与错"的定义也在不断地变化，法律也随之演变。人类未来的发展仍然离不开法律的力量！

People often fear the law and are perplexed by the "unrevealed secrecy" of the law. However, the real purpose of the law is to dispel people's fear of the unknown and to protect the stability of society. It is because of the law that we have today's civilization and prosperity.

The famous Austrian legal scholar Eugen Ehrlich once said, "the center of gravity of legal development lies not in legislation, nor in juristic science, nor in judicial decision, but in society itself." With the development of the times and the progress of science and technology, people's definition of "right or wrong" is constantly evolving—and so is the law. The future development of mankind is inevitably intertwined with the power of law!

图书在版编目(CIP)数据

成长的法律烦恼/沈奕,沈宏山著. —上海:复旦大学出版社,2020.10
ISBN 978-7-309-15264-7

Ⅰ.①成… Ⅱ.①沈…②沈… Ⅲ.①法律-中国-青少年读物 Ⅳ.①D920.5

中国版本图书馆 CIP 数据核字(2020)第 159537 号

成长的法律烦恼
沈 奕 沈宏山 著
责任编辑/方毅超

复旦大学出版社有限公司出版发行
上海市国权路 579 号 邮编:200433
网址:fupnet@fudanpress.com http://www.fudanpress.com
门市零售:86-21-65102580 团体订购:86-21-65104505
外埠邮购:86-21-65642846 出版部电话:86-21-65642845
上海盛通时代印刷有限公司

开本 850×1168 1/32 印张 10.125 字数 193 千
2020 年 10 月第 1 版第 1 次印刷

ISBN 978-7-309-15264-7/D·1060
定价:69.00 元

如有印装质量问题,请向复旦大学出版社有限公司出版部调换。
版权所有 侵权必究